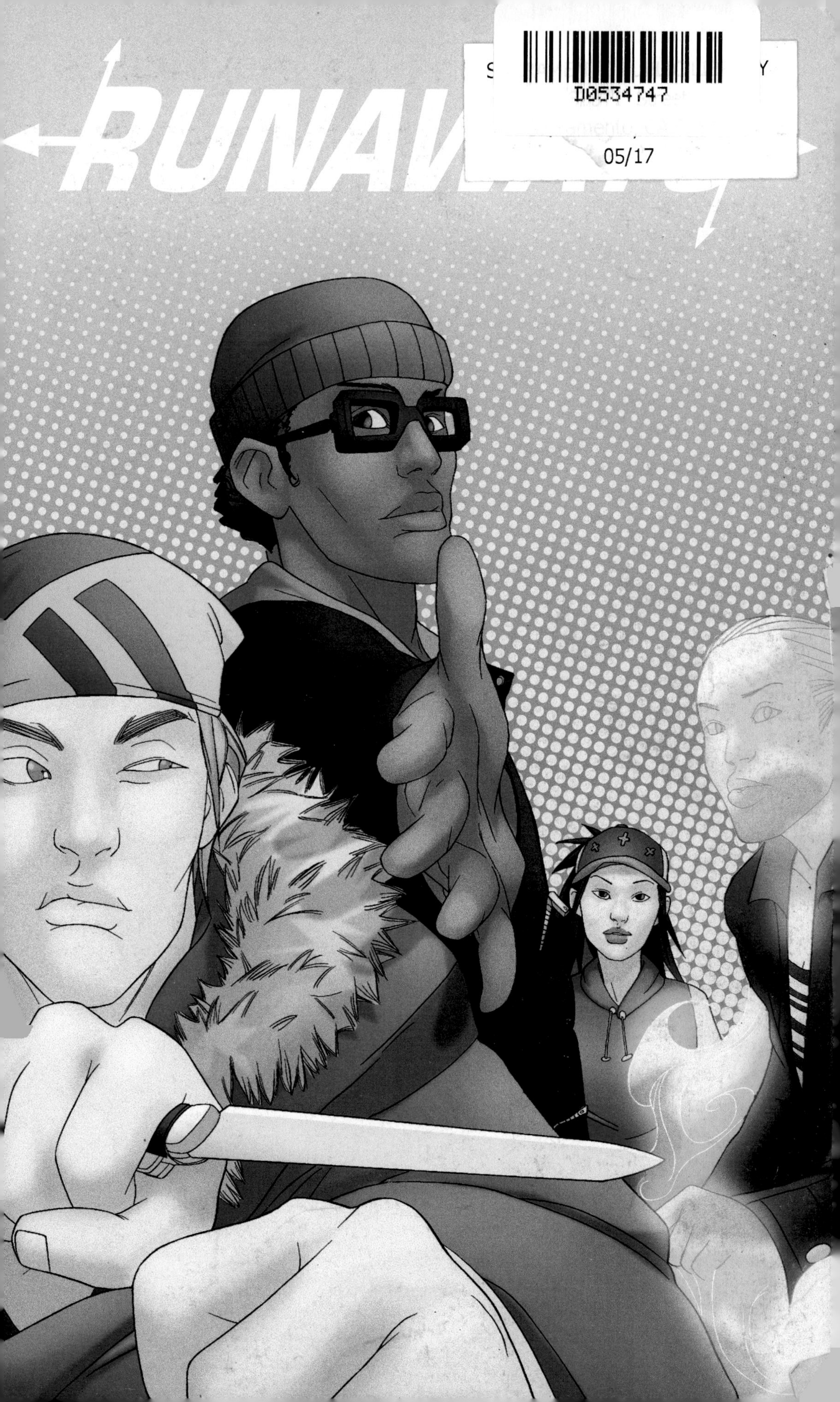

RUNAWAYS

WRITER: **BRIAN K. VAUGHAN**

PENCILS: **ADRIAN ALPHONA**

INKS: **CRAIG YEUNG**

COLORS: **CHRISTINA STRAIN**

LETTERS: **VC's RANDY GENTILE**

COVER ART: **JO CHEN**

ASSISTANT EDITOR: **MACKENZIE CADENHEAD**

EDITOR: **C.B. CEBULSKI**

RUNAWAYS CREATED BY **BRIAN K. VAUGHAN** & **ADRIAN ALPHONA**

COLLECTION EDITOR: JENNIFER GRÜNWALD • ASSISTANT EDITOR: CAITLIN O'CONNELL
ASSOCIATE MANAGING EDITOR: KATERI WOODY • EDITOR, SPECIAL PROJECTS: MARK D. BEAZLEY
VP PRODUCTION & SPECIAL PROJECTS: JEFF YOUNGQUIST • SVP PRINT, SALES & MARKETING: DAVID GABRIEL

EDITOR IN CHIEF: AXEL ALONSO • CHIEF CREATIVE OFFICER: JOE QUESADA
PRESIDENT: DAN BUCKLEY • EXECUTIVE PRODUCER: ALAN FINE

RUNAWAYS VOL. 3: THE GOOD DIE YOUNG. Contains material originally published in magazine form as RUNAWAYS #13-18. Second edition. First printing 2017. ISBN# 978-1-302-90501-9. Published by MARVEL WORLDWIDE, INC., a subsidiary of MARVEL ENTERTAINMENT, LLC. OFFICE OF PUBLICATION: 135 West 50th Street, New York, NY 10020. Copyright © 2017 MARVEL No similarity between any of the names, characters, persons, and/or institutions in this magazine with those of any living or dead person or institution is intended, and any such similarity which may exist is purely coincidental. **Printed in the U.S.A.** DAN BUCKLEY, President, Marvel Entertainment; JOE QUESADA, Chief Creative Officer; TOM BREVOORT, SVP of Publishing; DAVID BOGART, SVP of Business Affairs & Operations, Publishing & Partnership; C.B. CEBULSKI, VP of Brand Management & Development, Asia; DAVID GABRIEL, SVP of Sales & Marketing, Publishing; JEFF YOUNGQUIST, VP of Production & Special Projects; DAN CARR, Executive Director of Publishing Technology; ALEX MORALES, Director of Publishing Operations; SUSAN CRESPI, Production Manager; STAN LEE, Chairman Emeritus. For information regarding advertising in Marvel Comics or on Marvel.com, please contact Vit DeBellis, Integrated Sales Manager, at vdebellis@marvel.com. For Marvel subscription inquiries, please call 888-511-5480. **Manufactured between 2/17/2017 and 3/21/2017 by QUAD/GRAPHICS WASECA, WASECA, MN, USA.**

10 9 8 7 6 5 4 3 2 1

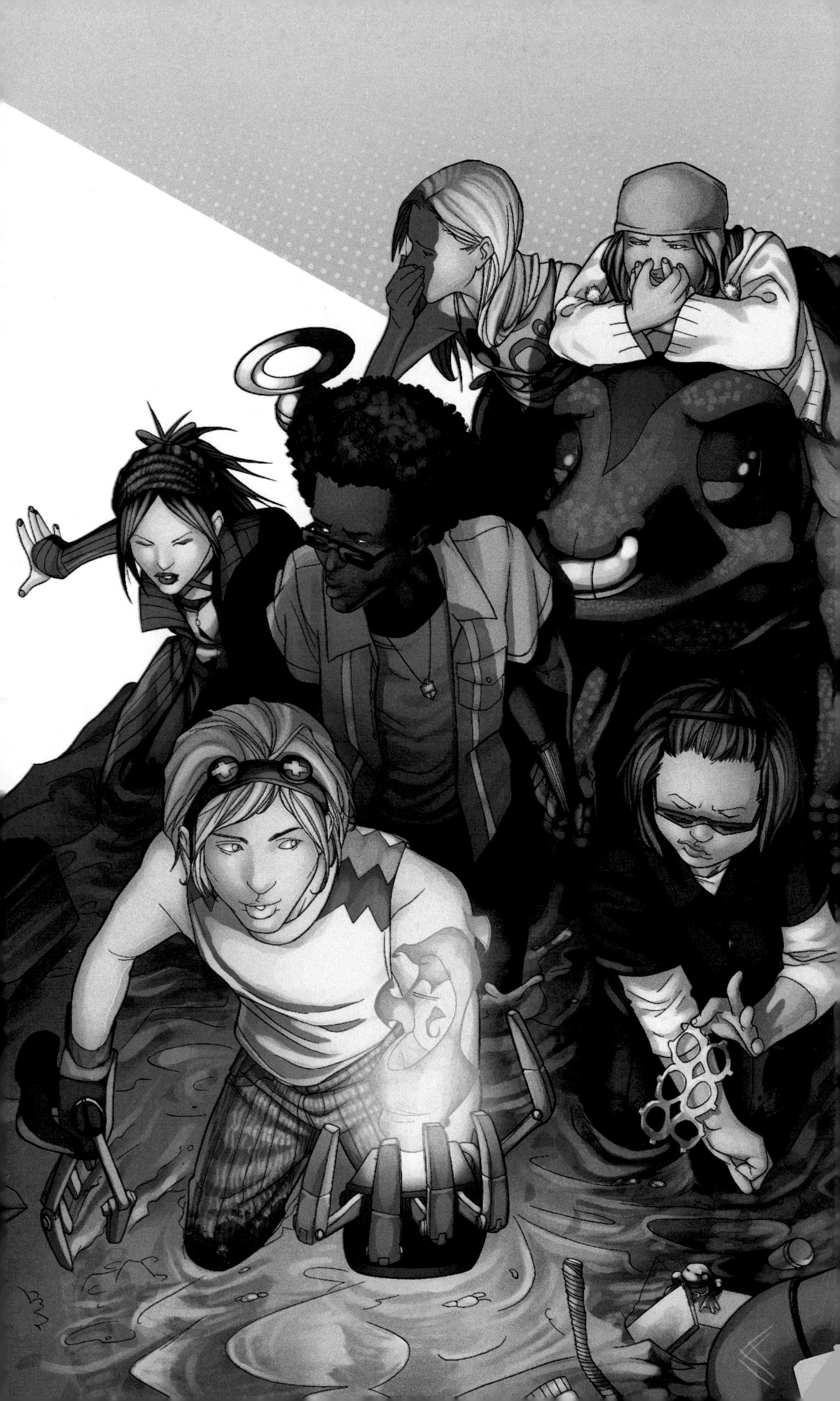

PREVIOUSLY:

TEENAGER ALEX WILDER AND FIVE OTHER ONLY CHILDREN ALWAYS THOUGHT THAT THEIR PARENTS WERE BORING LOS ANGELES SOCIALITES, UNTIL THE KIDS WITNESS THE ADULTS MURDER A YOUNG GIRL IN SOME KIND OF DARK SACRIFICIAL RITUAL. THE TEENS SOON LEARN THAT THEIR PARENTS ARE PART OF A SECRET ORGANIZATION CALLED "THE PRIDE," A COLLECTION OF CRIME BOSSES, TIME-TRAVELING DESPOTS, ALIEN OVERLORDS, MAD SCIENTISTS, EVIL MUTANTS AND DARK WIZARDS.

AFTER STEALING WEAPONS AND RESOURCES FROM THESE VILLAINOUS ADULTS (INCLUDING AN ENCRYPTED BOOK ABOUT THE PRIDE, A MYSTICAL DECODER RING AND A PSYCHIC VELOCIRAPTOR NAMED OLD LACE), THE KIDS RUN AWAY FROM HOME AND VOW TO BRING THEIR PARENTS TO JUSTICE. BUT WITH THE HELP OF OPERATIVES IN THE LAPD, THE PRIDE FRAMES THEIR CHILDREN FOR THE MURDER THEY COMMITTED, AND THE FUGITIVE RUNAWAYS ARE FORCED TO RETREAT TO A SUBTERRANEAN HIDEOUT. USING THE DIVERSE POWERS AND SKILLS THEY INHERITED, THE KIDS NOW HOPE TO ATONE FOR THEIR PARENTS' CRIMES BY HELPING THOSE IN NEED.

BUT THE PRIDE HAS OTHER PLANS FOR THEIR CHILDREN...

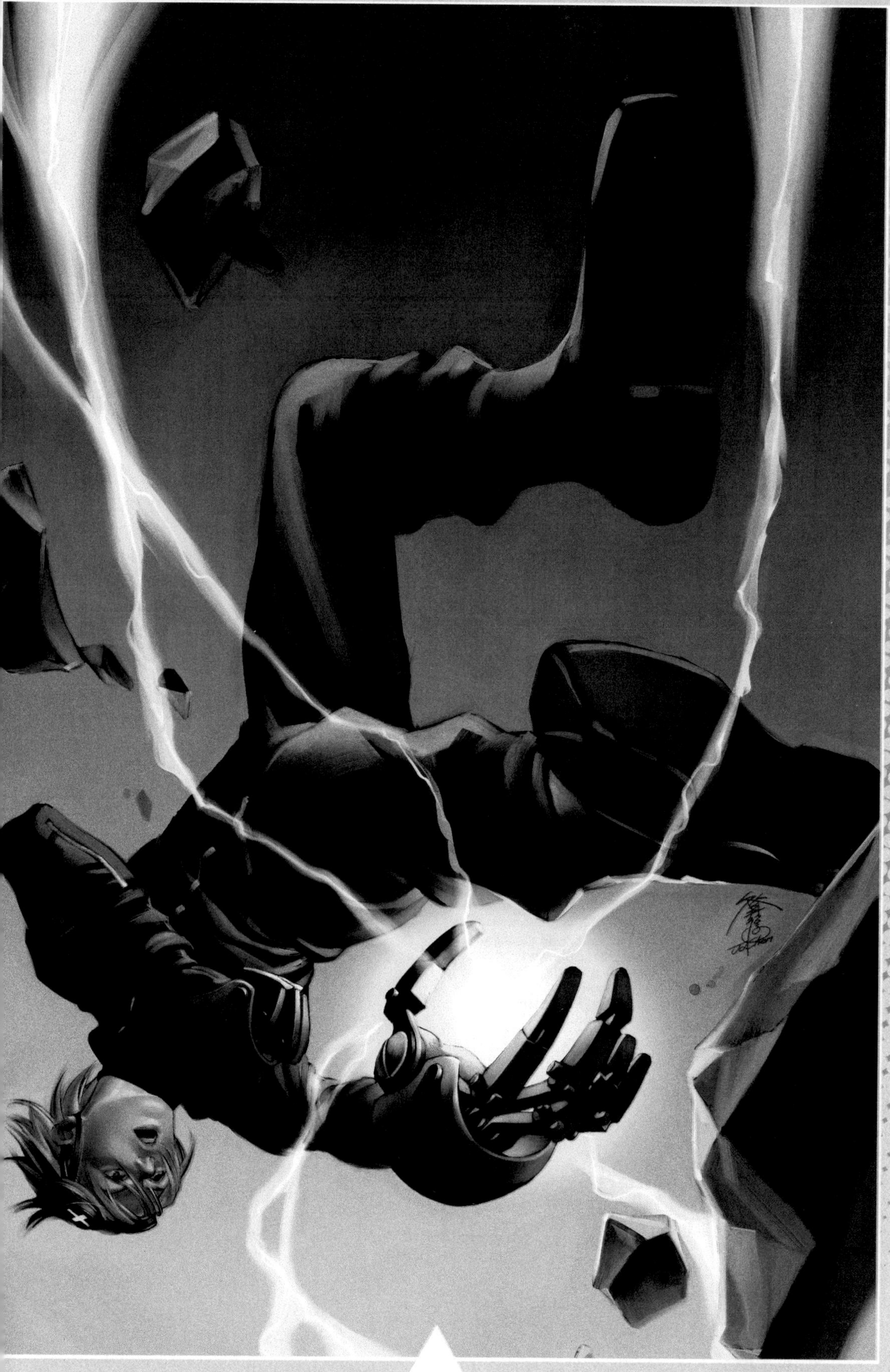

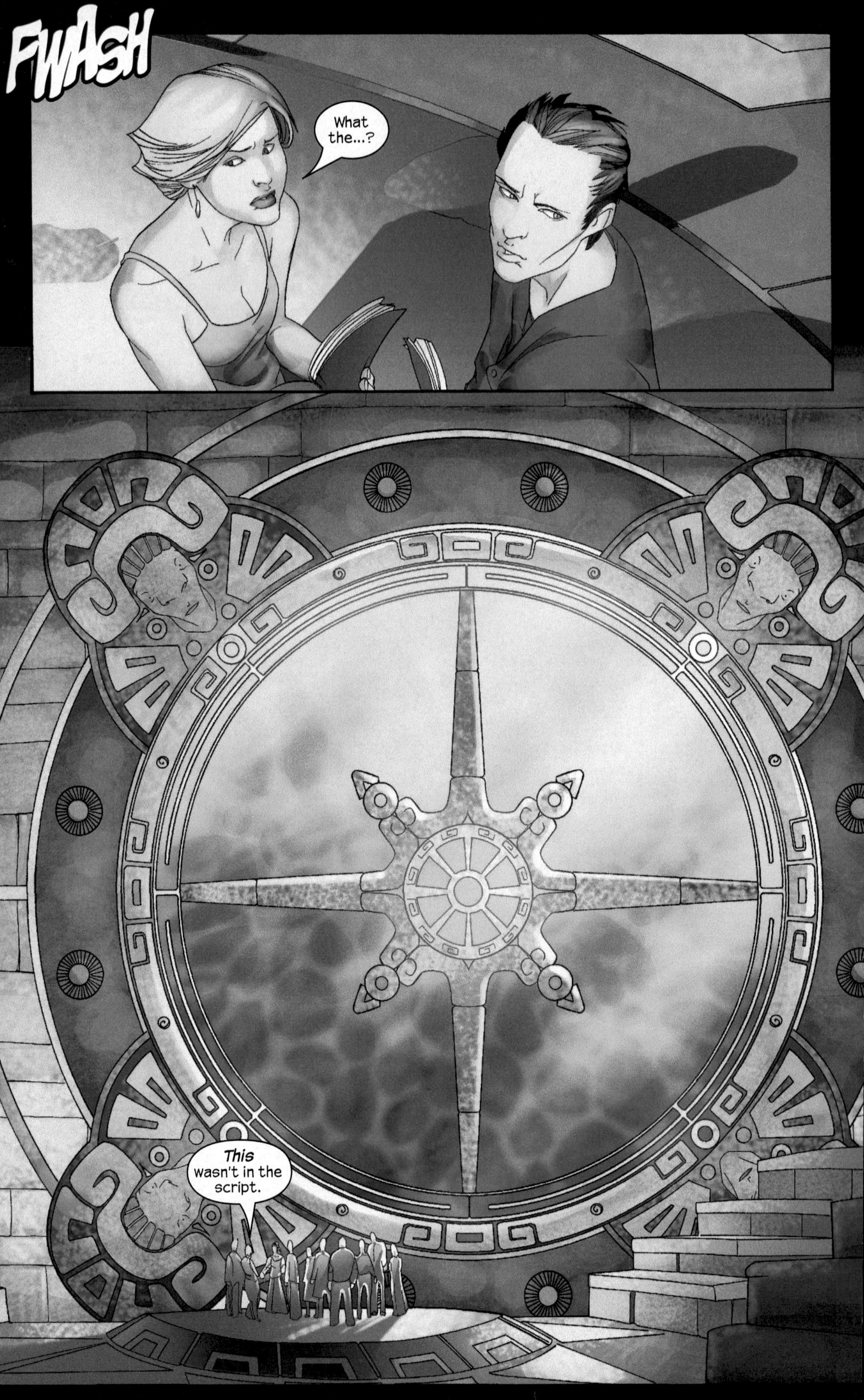
FWASH
What the...?
This wasn't in the script.

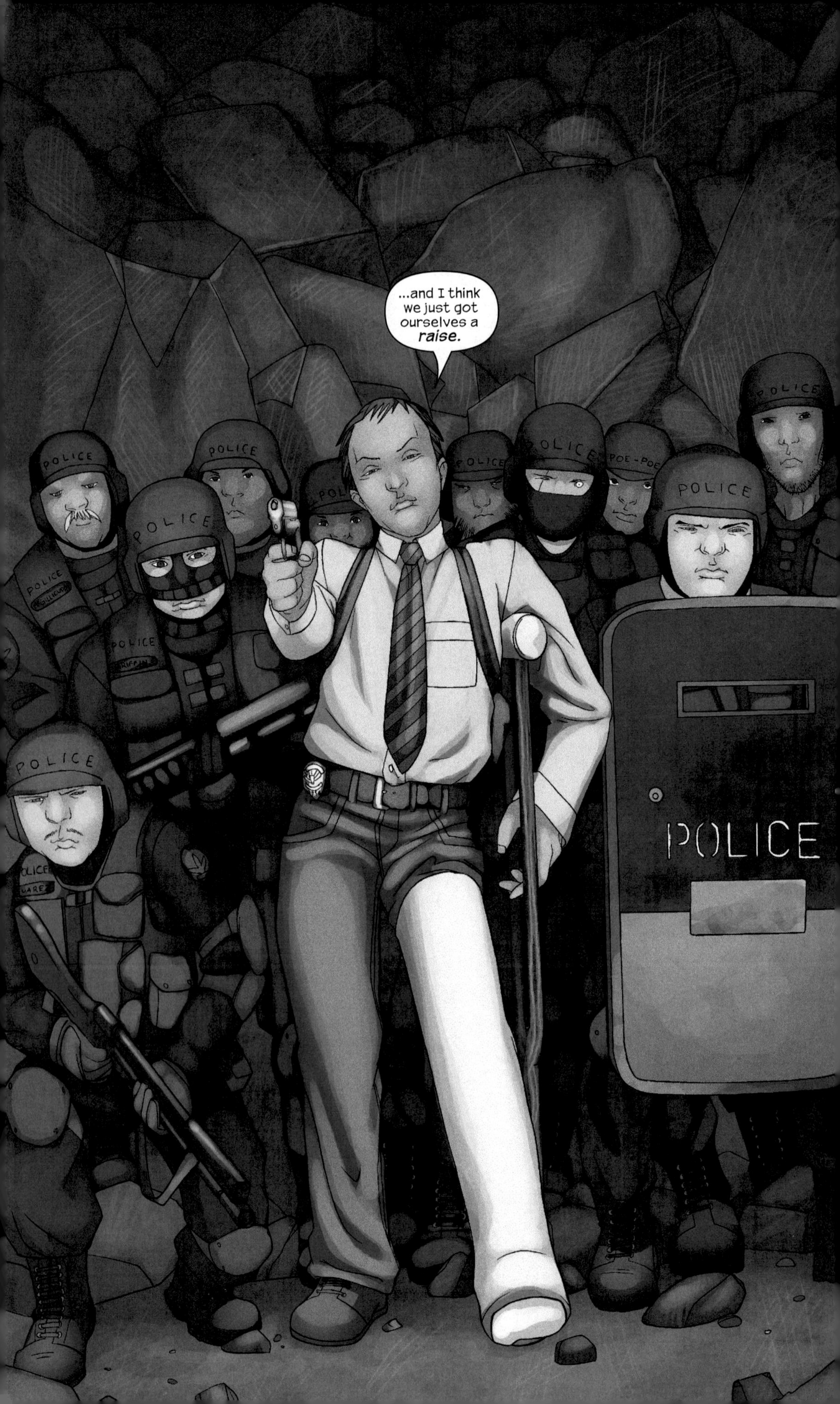
...and I think we just got ourselves a *raise.*
POLICE

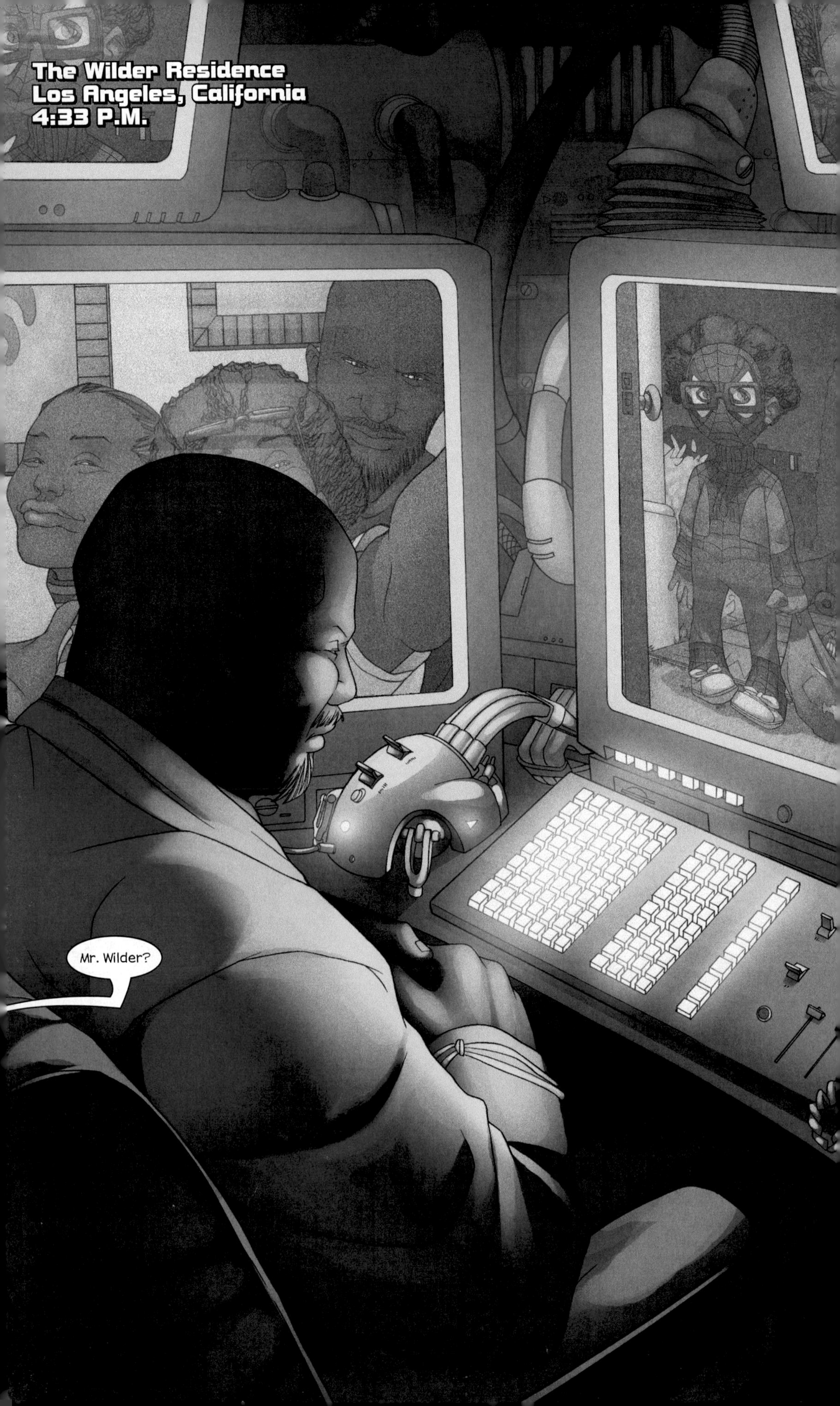
The Wilder Residence
Los Angeles, California
4:33 P.M.
Mr. Wilder?

But it was *years* ago that we agreed to donate our chance at immortality to those six kids. Back then, none of us imagined that we would ever *want* to live forever.

The twelve of us joined The Pride because we each wanted one of the Gibborim's six tickets to paradise for *ourselves.*

We *never* would have given up that shot at eternal life if my wife hadn't become *pregnant...* if *all* of us hadn't decided that we needed *little ones* to share our empty mansions with.

Surviving to an age like *forty* sounded like an eternity already, more than enough time to enjoy all the Gibborim had granted us.

But now we're *old men,* rapidly approaching the Final Wave, and the ungrateful brats we sacrificed everything for have *abandoned* us.

Admit it, some nights, you think about *letting* your son perish with the rest of this wretched populace... and taking his spot in the Next World for *yourself.*

NEVER!

≺hkk≻

I have done *terrible* things in my life, but for the last sixteen years, I have been confident that I was doing them for a *noble* reason.

I am going to find Alex and give him what is rightfully his, and I will *destroy* anyone who stands in my way.

...thank... you.

What did you say?

Thank you... for saying what I wanted to hear. My son and I have had our differences, but I love Chase more than life itself. *Literally.*

My wife and I feel the exact same way that you do, but I needed to be *certain* that we were all on the same page.

You were *testing* me?

Geoffrey, be rational. We're a group of thieves and... and *murderers.* I've never trusted *any* of--

Stand by... my wife programmed our chronometers to scan police radios for certain *key* phrases.

Apparently, a patrolman just received an anonymous tip about a white van like my *son's* parked in Bronson Canyon.

Then we have to move *now...* before one of our overzealous agents decides to take matters into his *own* hands.

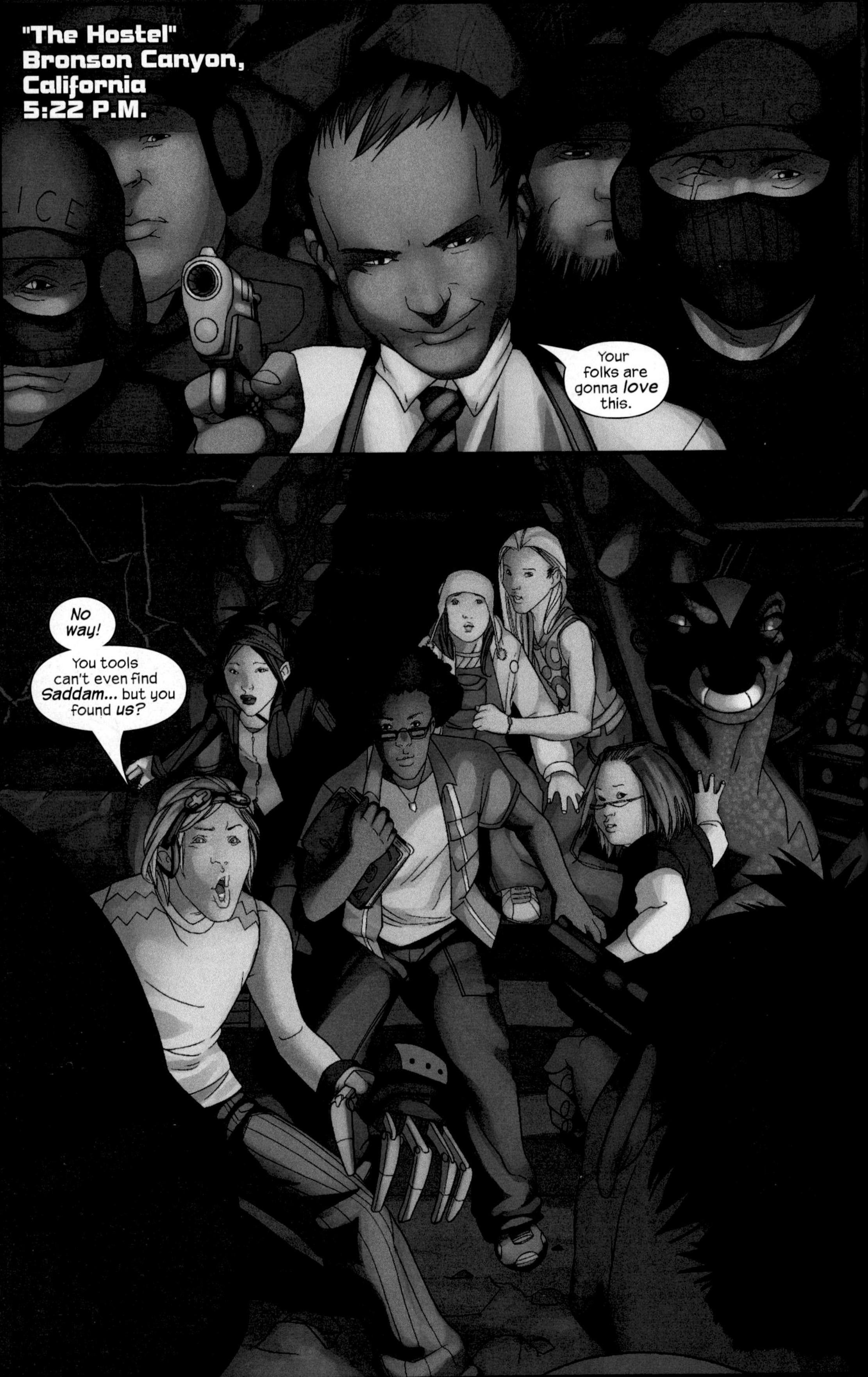
"The Hostel"
Bronson Canyon, California
5:22 P.M.
Your folks are gonna love this.
No way!
You tools can't even find Saddam... but you found us?

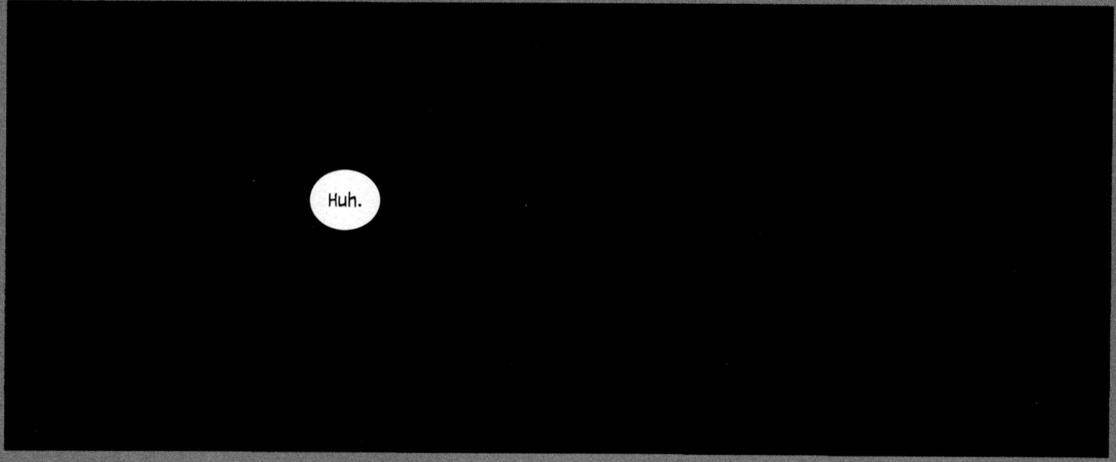
Huh.

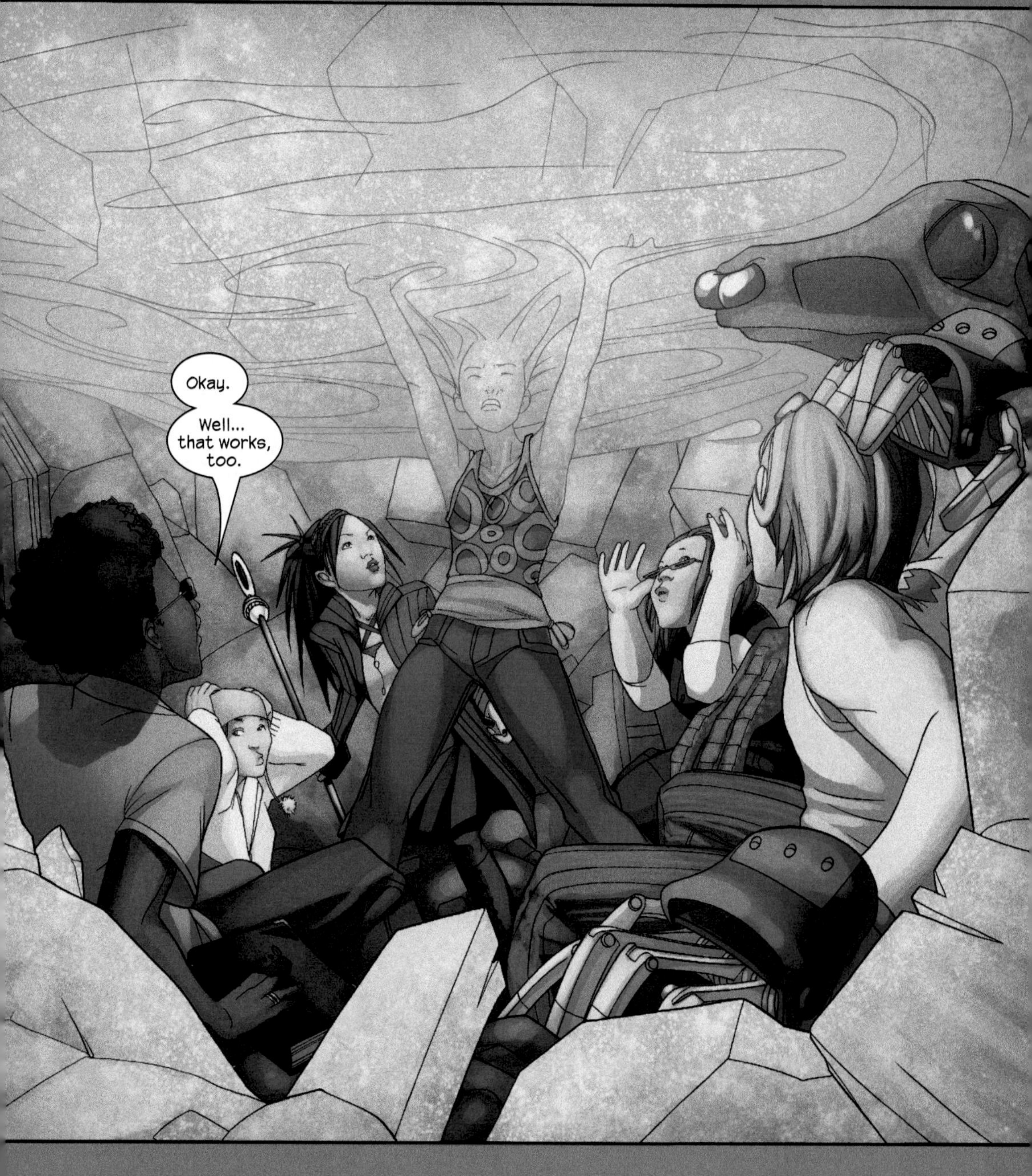
Okay.
Well... that works, too.

If it wasn't for the smell...

...this would sorta be *awesome*.

What the devil is taking them so long?

Don't get your spacesuit in a bunch, Mrs. Dean. They'll *be* here.

When? The last time we were late, the Gibborim threatened to send us to--

Calm yourself, Leslie.

The gang's all here.

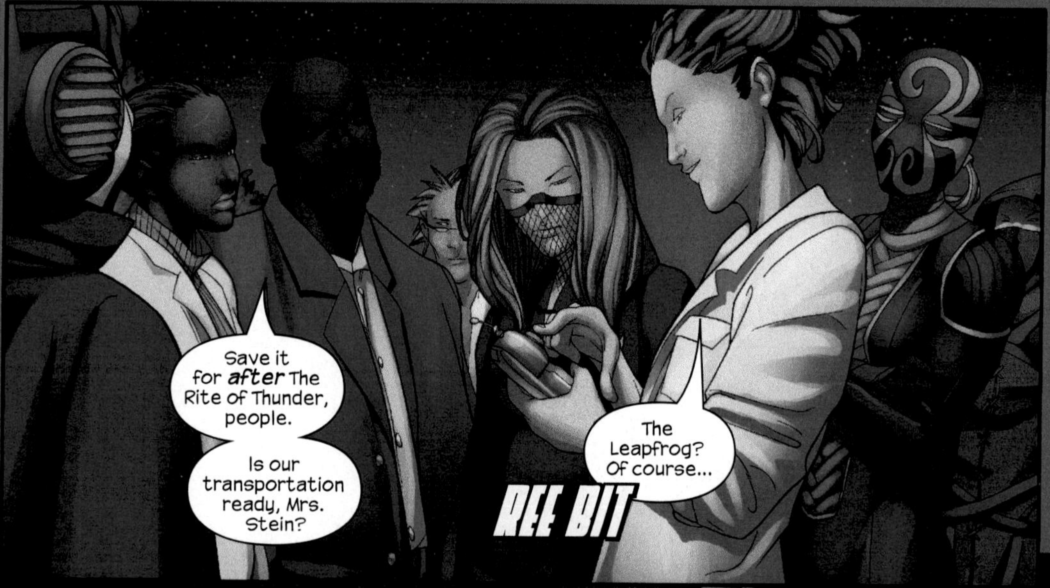
Save it for after The Rite of Thunder, people.
Is our transportation ready, Mrs. Stein?
The Leapfrog? Of course...
REE BIT

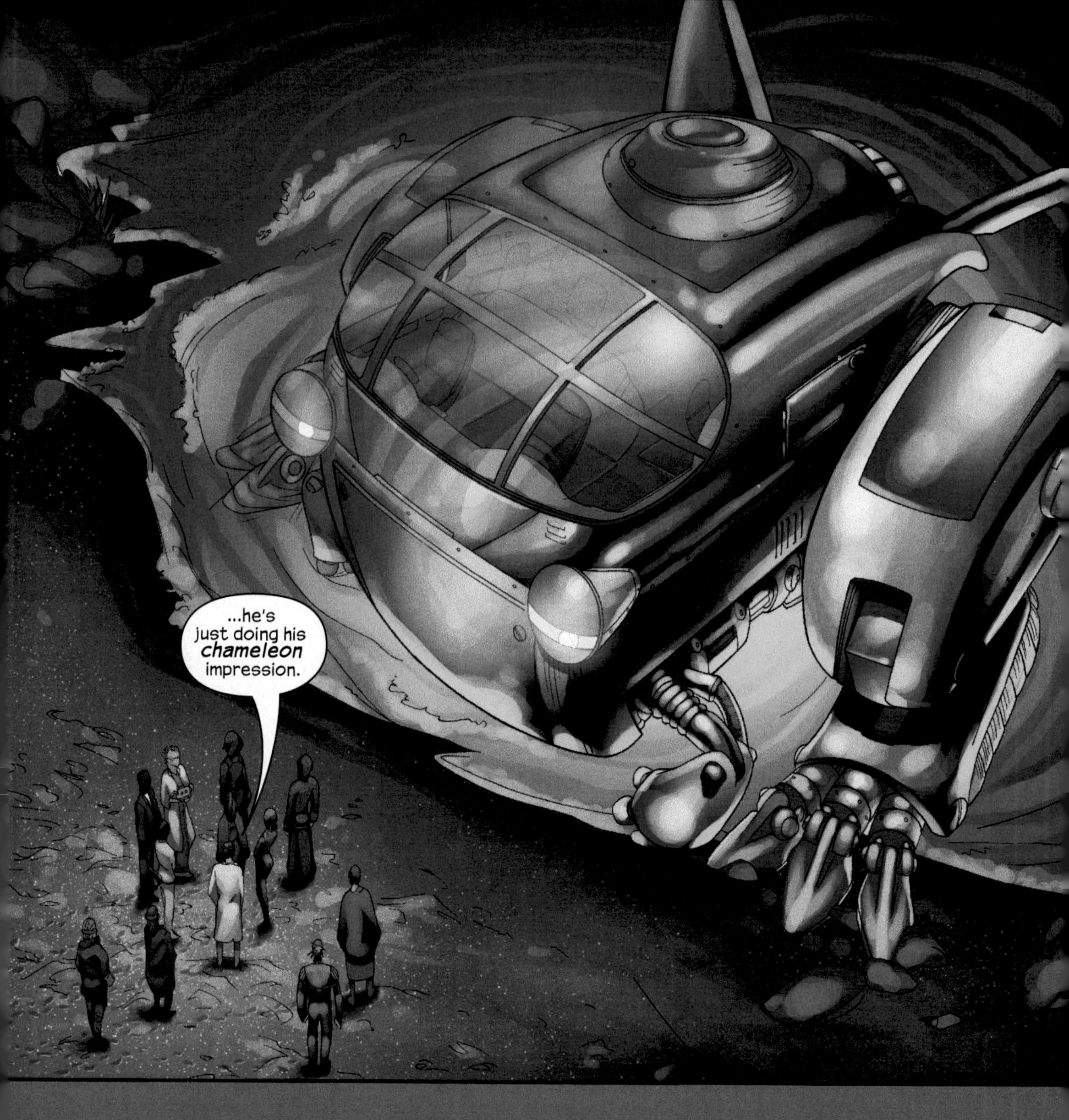
...he's just doing his chameleon impression.

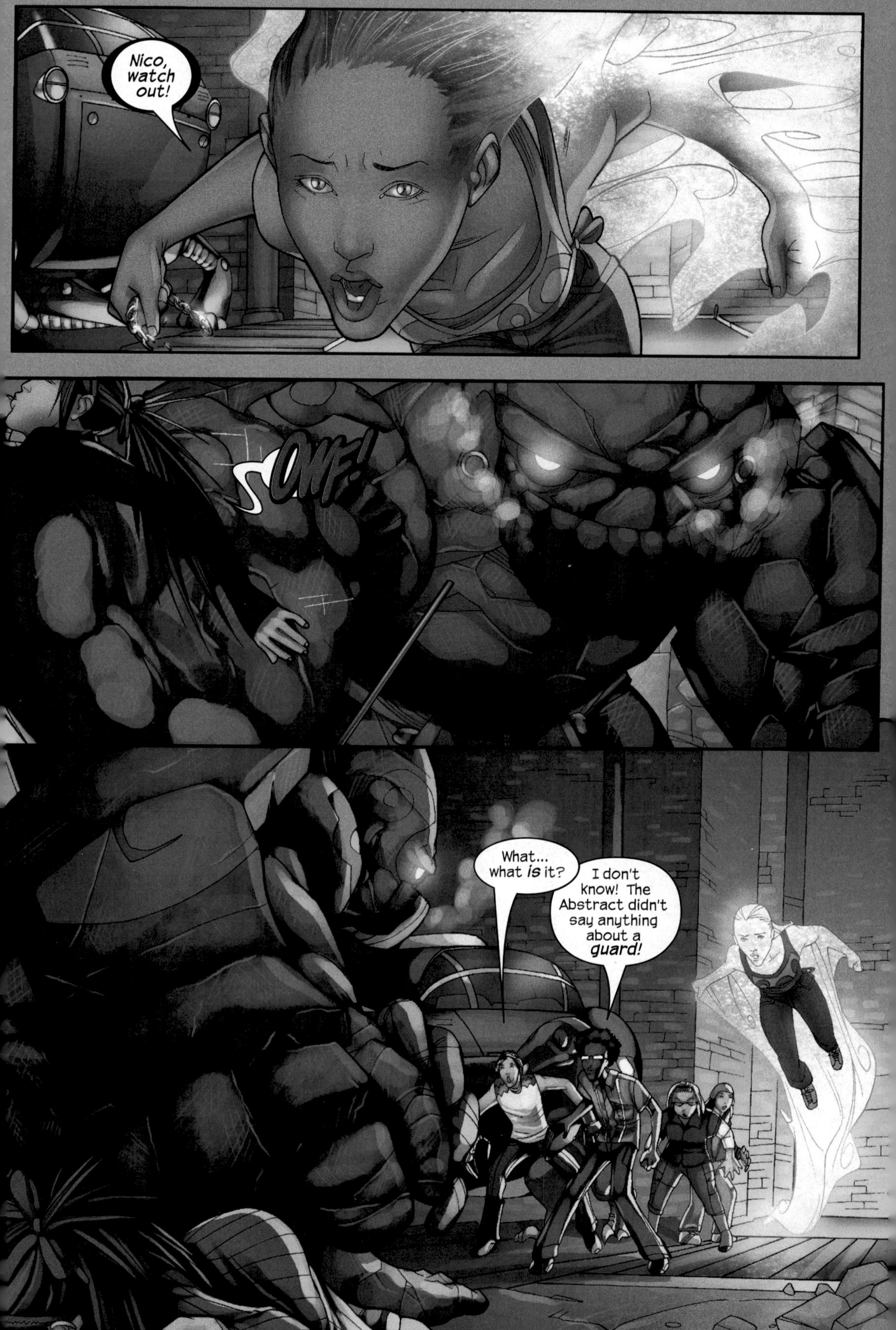

Nico, watch out!
SOWF!
What... what *is* it?
I don't know! The Abstract didn't say anything about a **guard!**

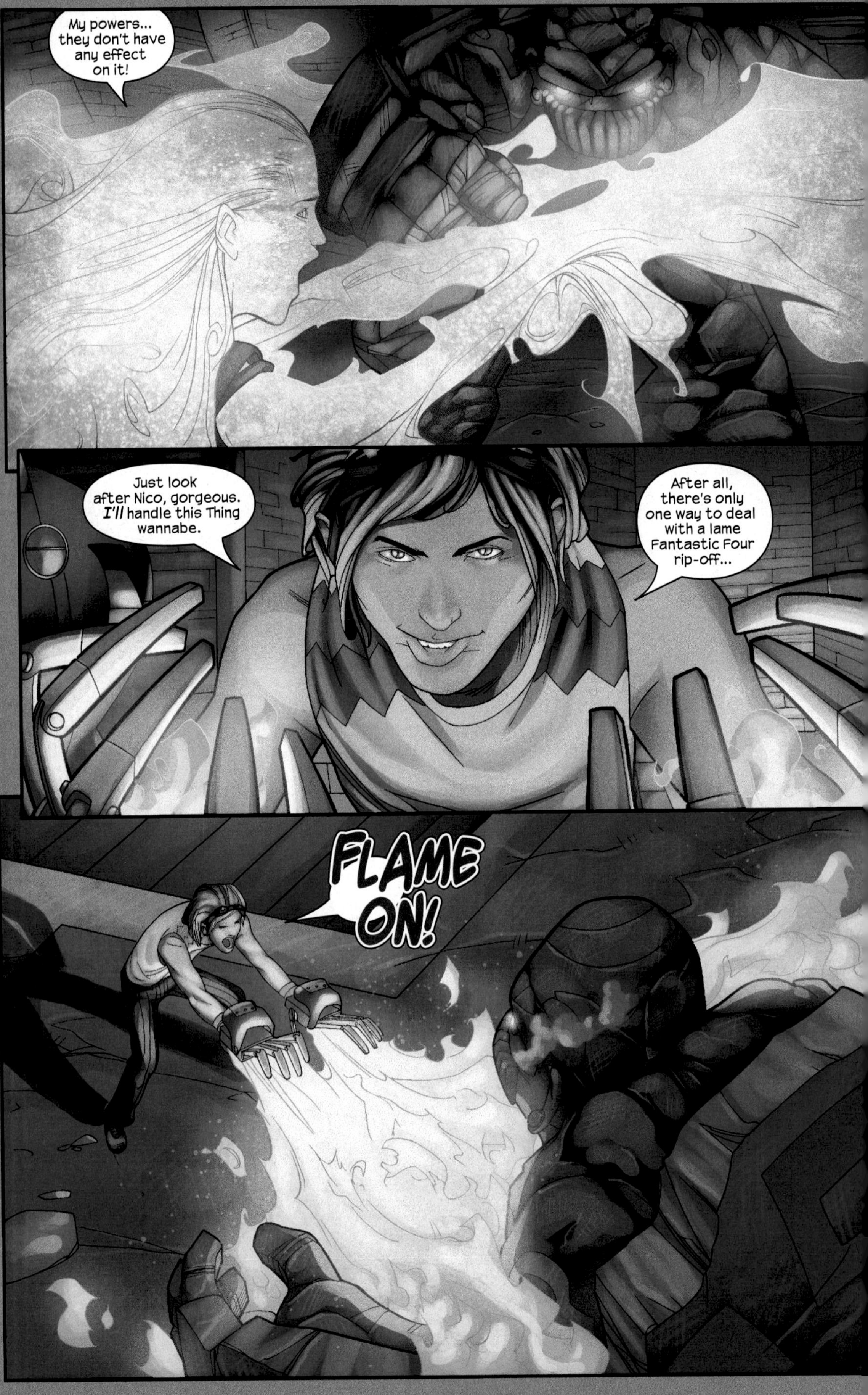
My powers... they don't have any effect on it!
Just look after Nico, gorgeous. *I'll* handle this Thing wannabe.
After all, there's only one way to deal with a lame Fantastic Four rip-off...
FLAME ON!

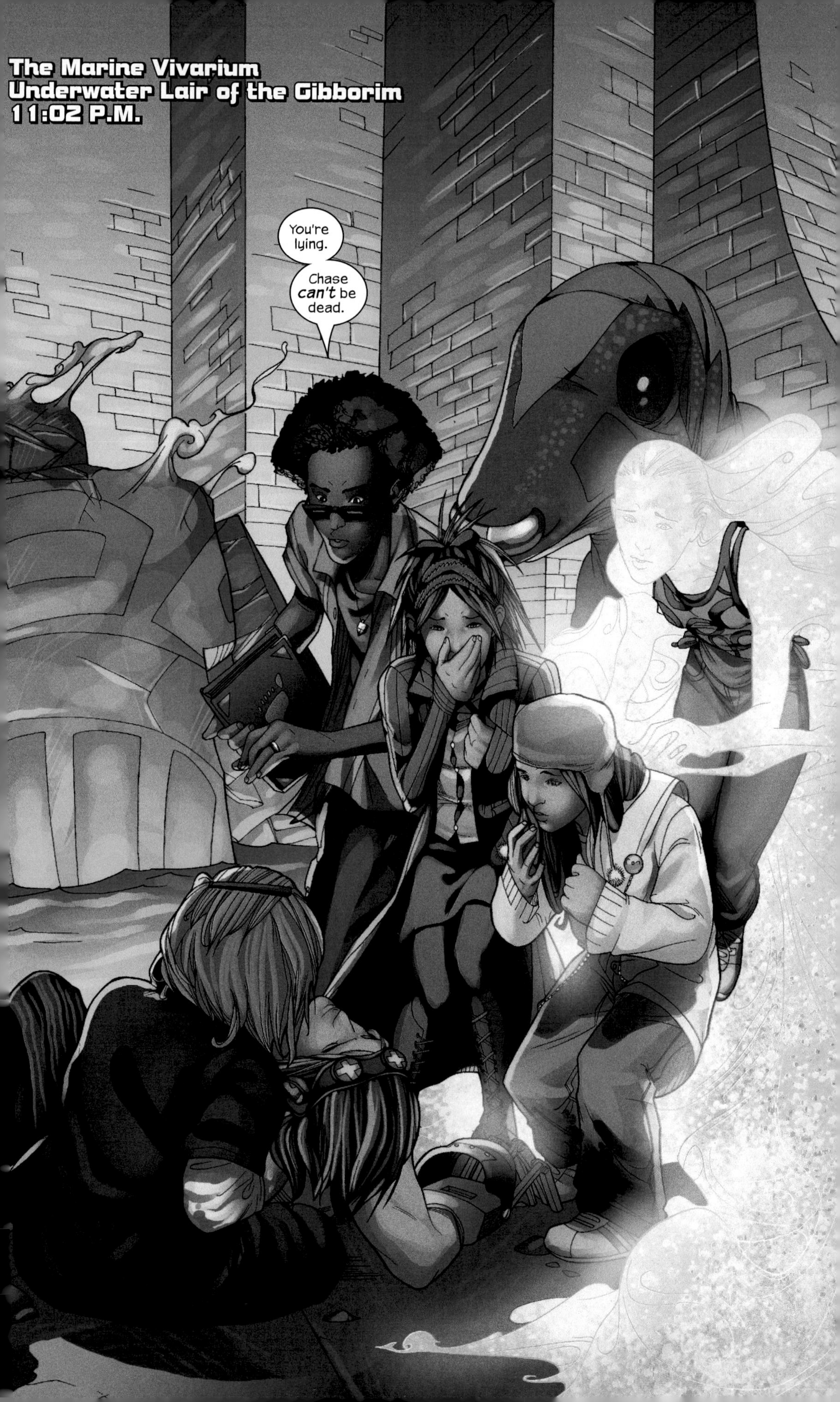
The Marine Vivarium
Underwater Lair of the Gibborim
11:02 P.M.
You're lying.
Chase can't be dead.

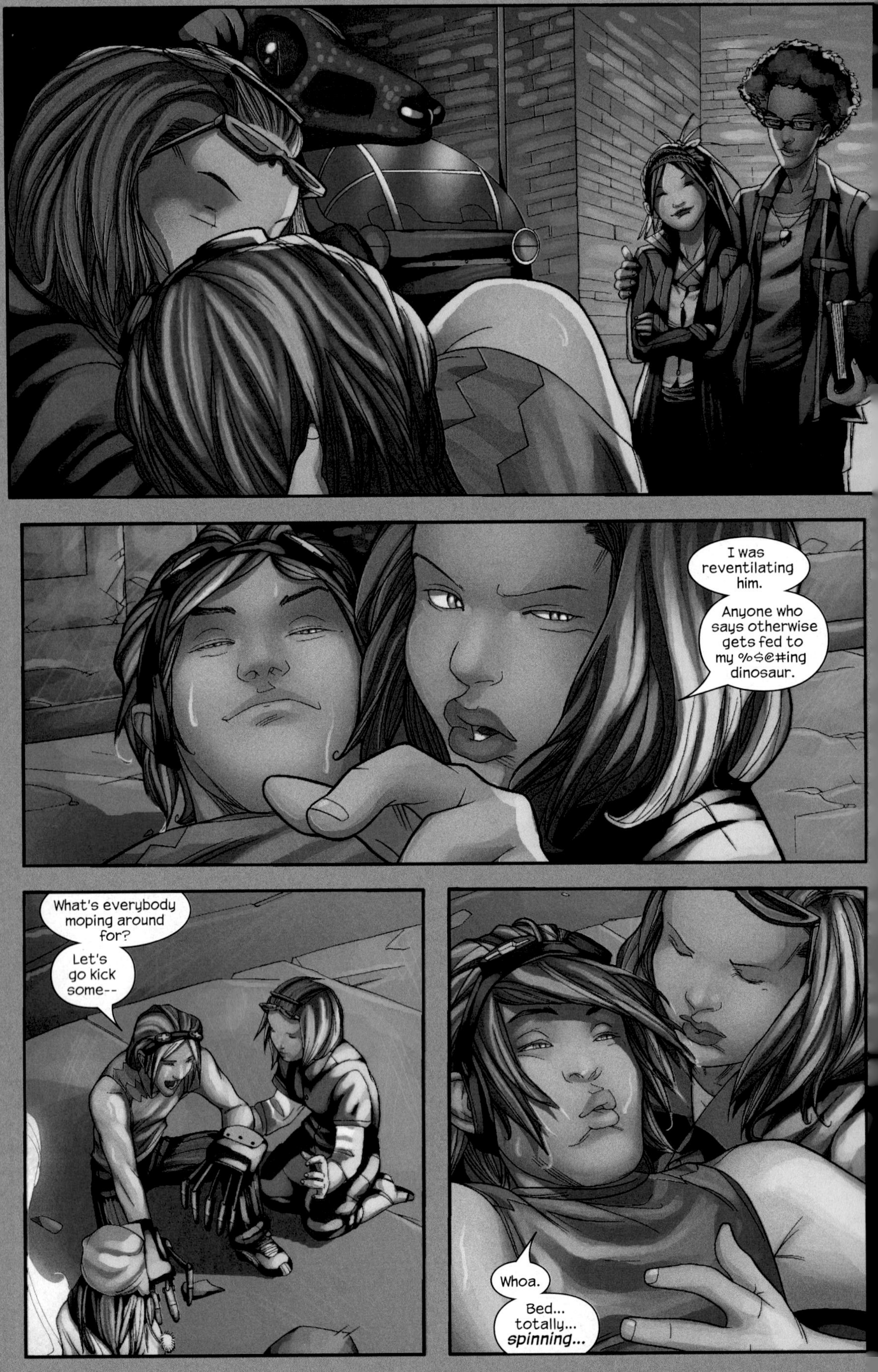
I was reventilating him.
Anyone who says otherwise gets fed to my %$€#ing dinosaur.
What's everybody moping around for?
Let's go kick some--
Whoa.
Bed... totally... *spinning...*

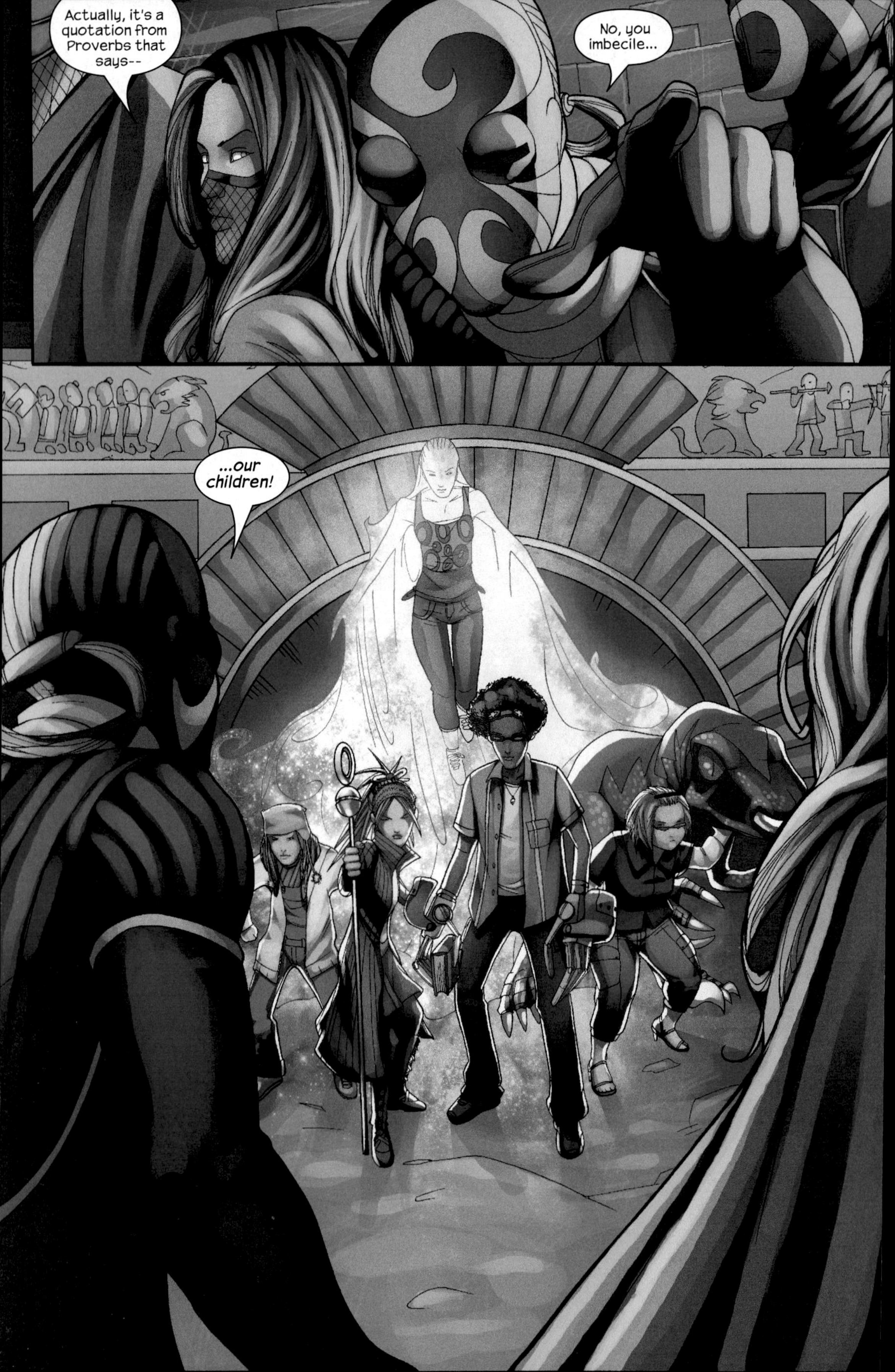
Actually, it's a quotation from Proverbs that says--
No, you imbecile...
...our children!

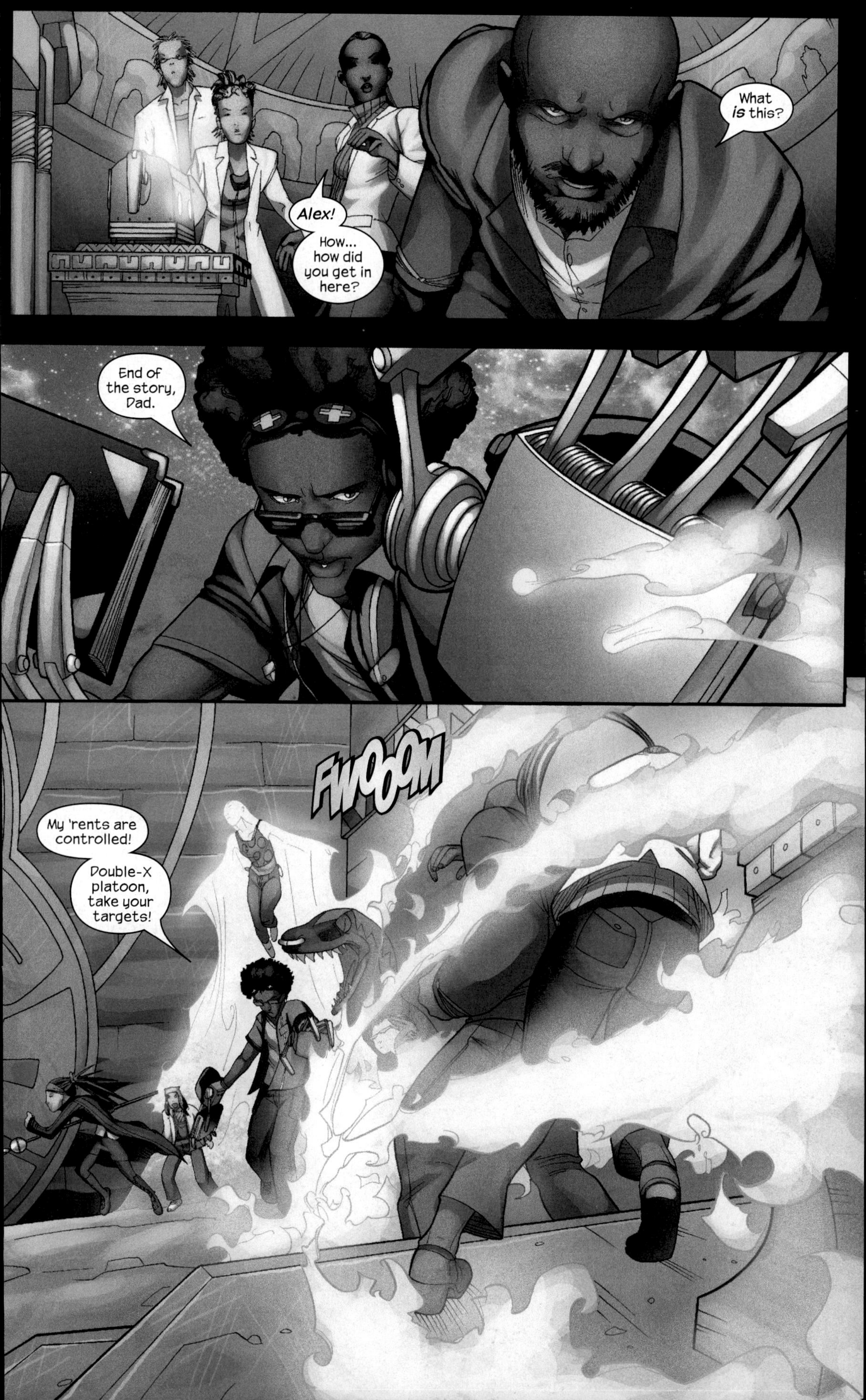
What *is* this?
Alex!
How... how did you get in here?
End of the story, Dad.
FWOOOM
My 'rents are controlled!
Double-X platoon, take your targets!

Remember the plan, girl.

If anything happens to me, you take your marching orders from *Alex.*

RRRRRR

Lovely to see you again, Gertrude... but I believe we've been through this routine before.

Your little pet is physically *incapable* of harming your dear old mum and me.

Be cool, babe.

You *know* our family's powers don't work on each other, Karolina.

Ready?

Set.

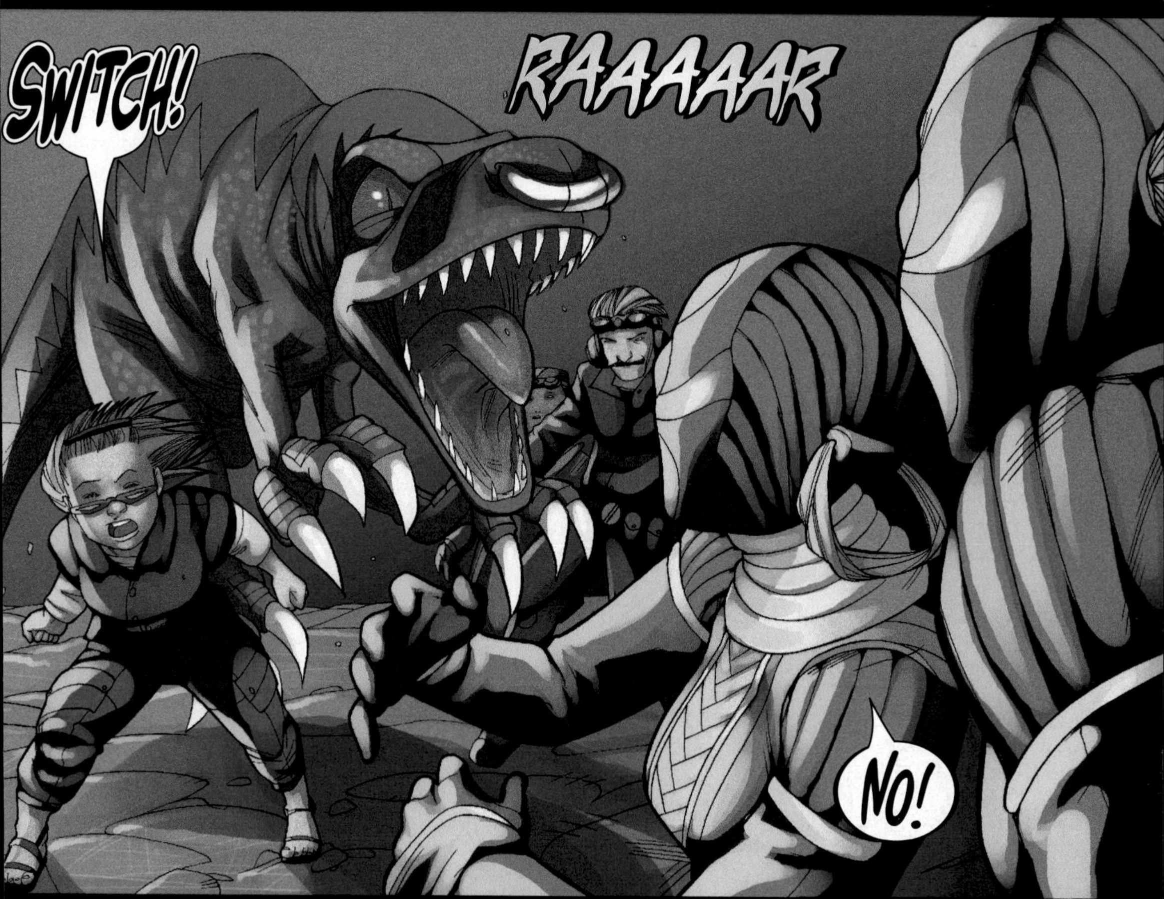
SWITCH!
RAAAAAR
NO!

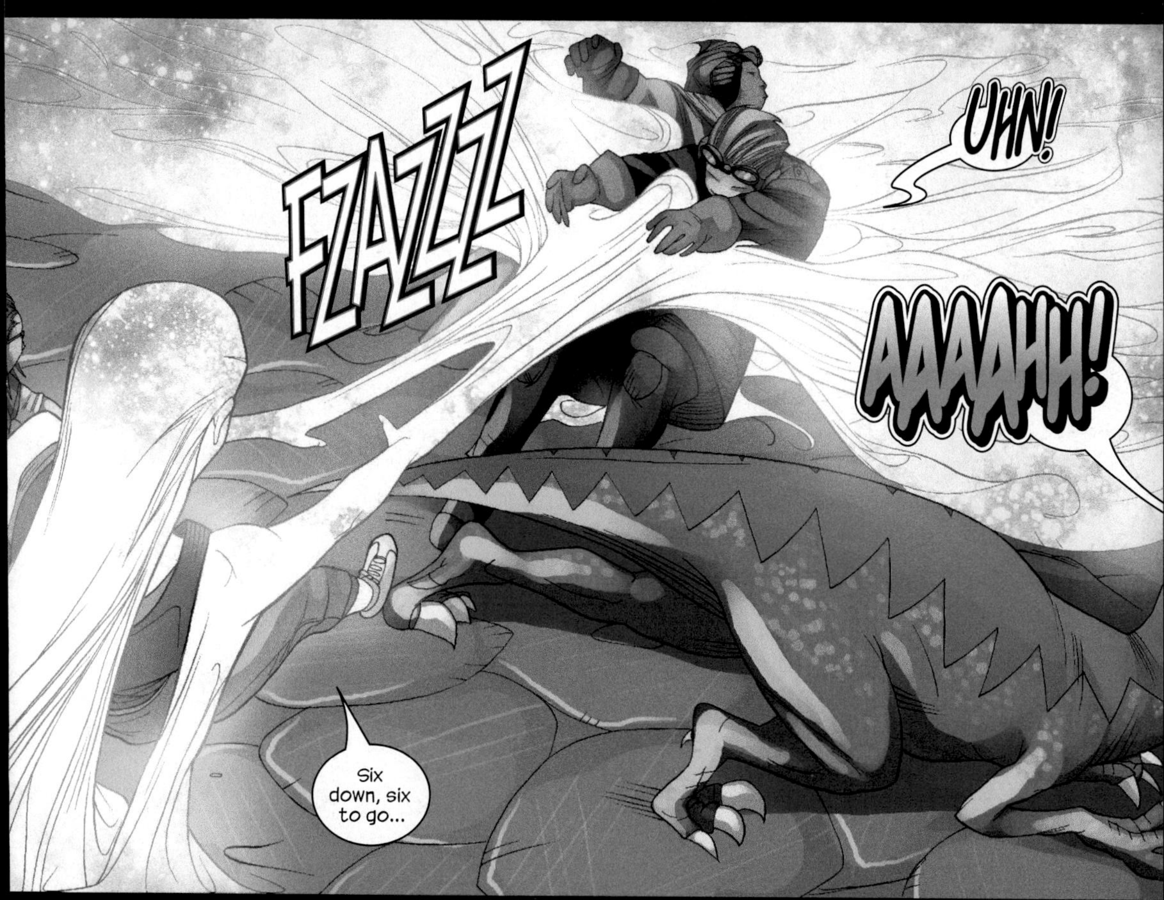
FZAZZZ
UHN!
AAAAHH!
Six down, six to go...

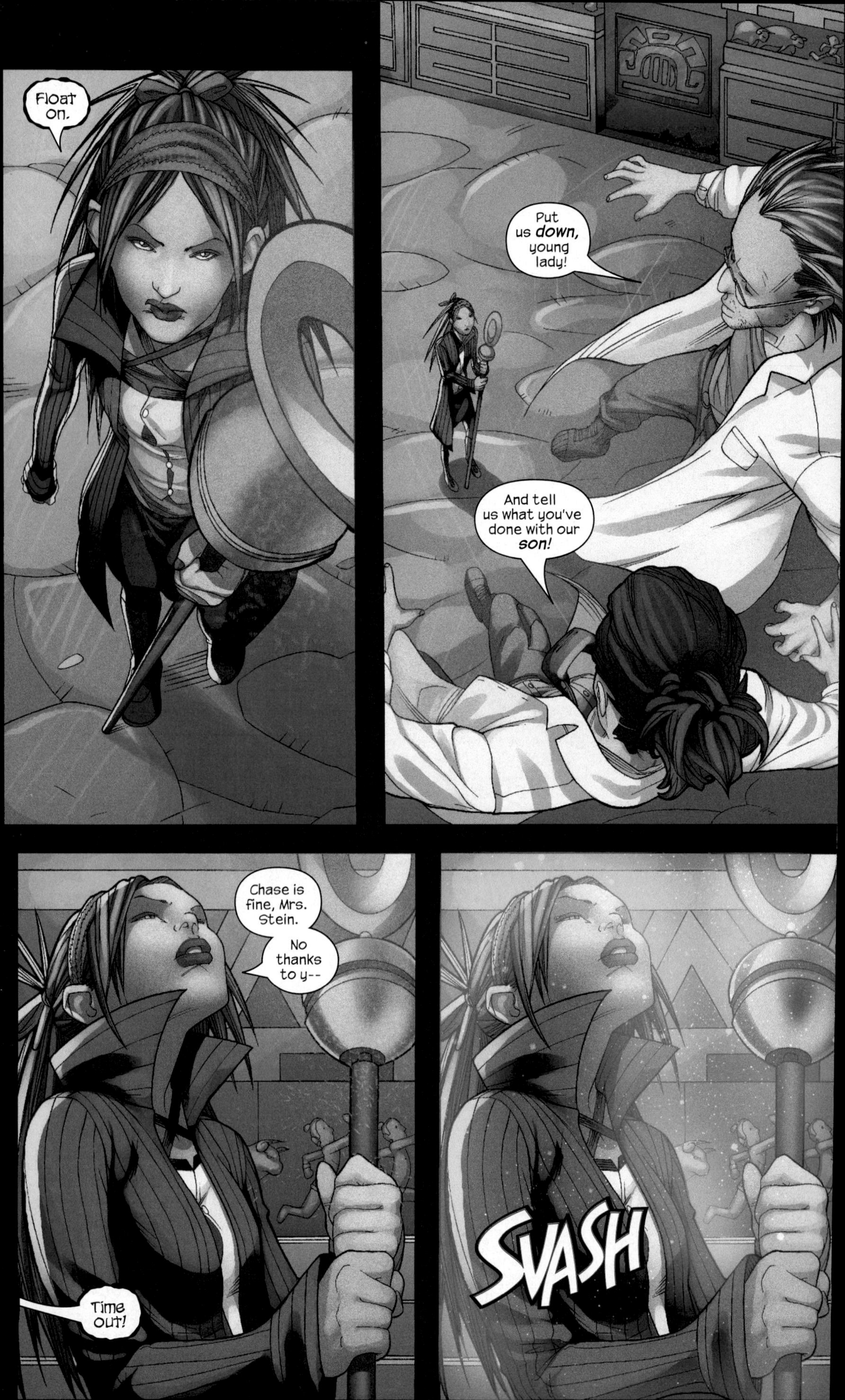
Float on.
Put us down, young lady!
And tell us what you've done with our son!
Chase is fine, Mrs. Stein.
No thanks to y--
Time out!
SVASH

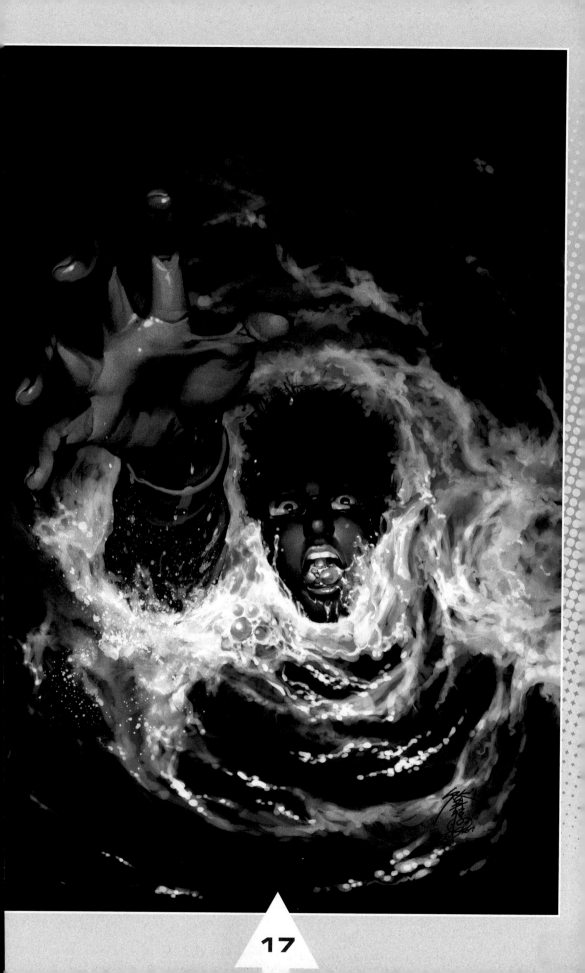

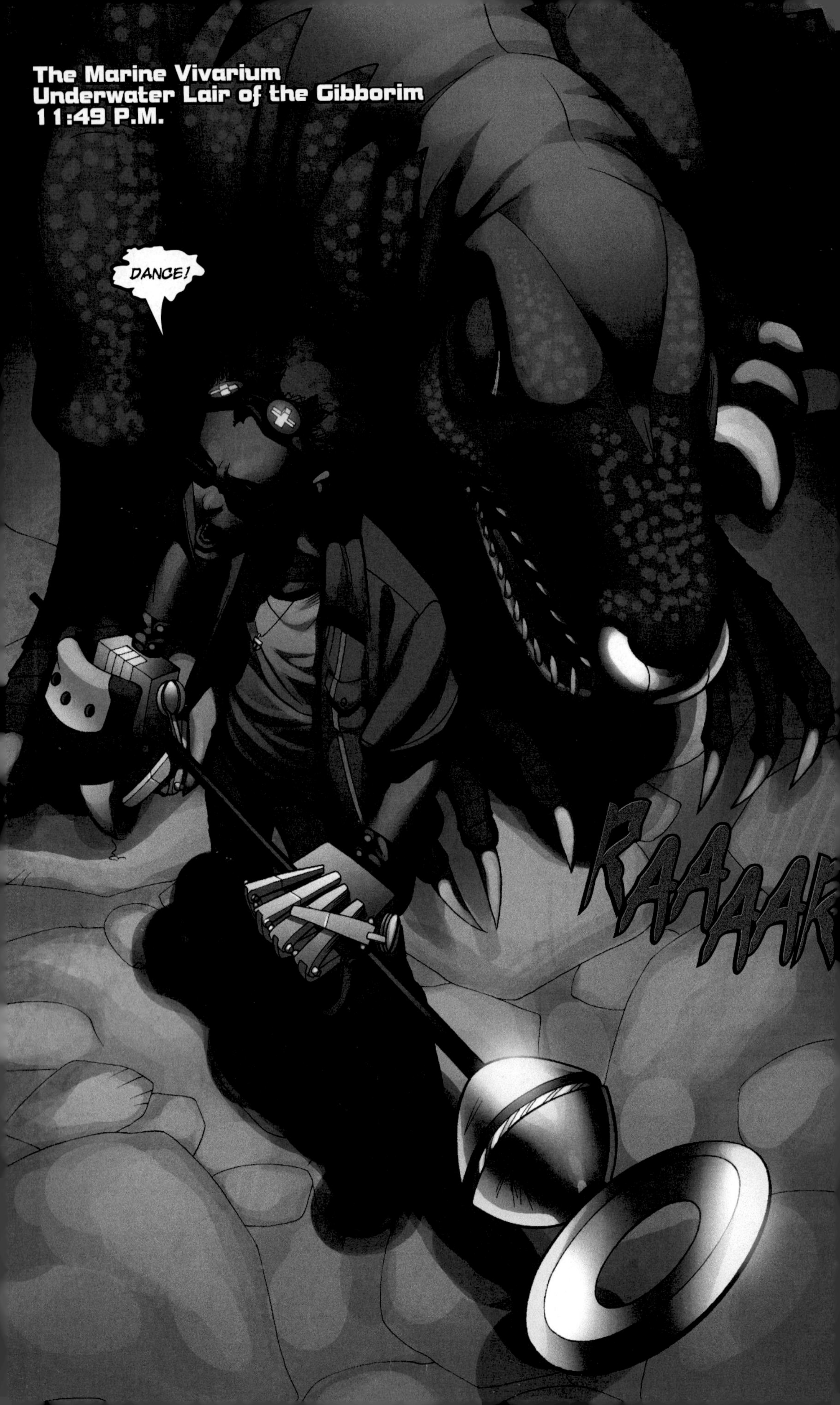
The Marine Vivarium
Underwater Lair of the Gibborim
11:49 P.M.
DANCE!
RAAAAR

Wha... what happened?

I've got to give you credit, Nico. You always made using this thing look *easy*.

I had to try a zillion different phrases before the Staff of One finally *unfroze* you from that *Girl, Interrupted* spell your mom and dad--

Alex, **look out!**

Your parents are right behind you!

I know.

They always have been.

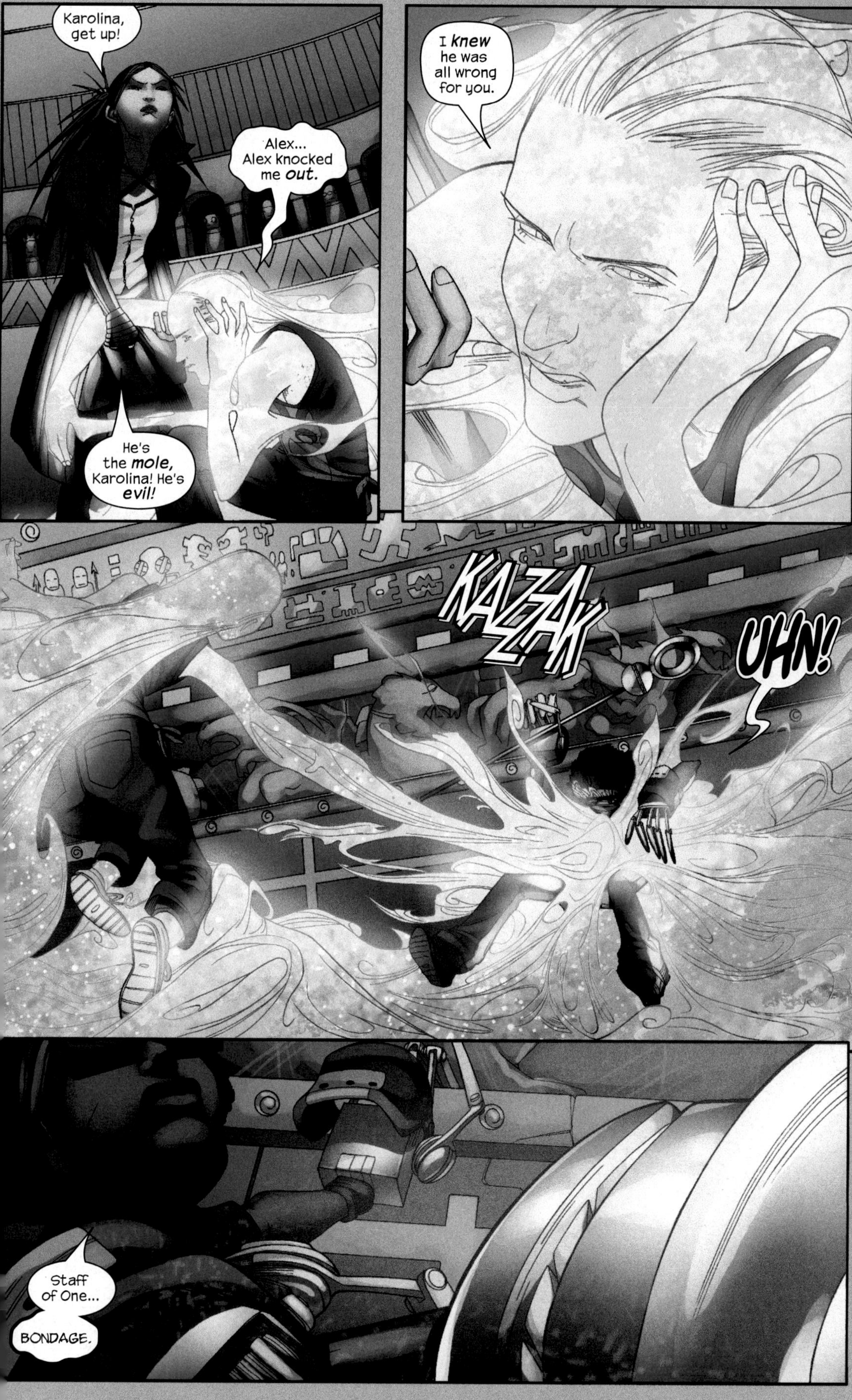
Karolina, get up!
Alex... Alex knocked me *out.*
He's the *mole,* Karolina! He's *evil!*
I *knew* he was all wrong for you.
KAZZAK
UHN!
Staff of One...
BONDAGE.

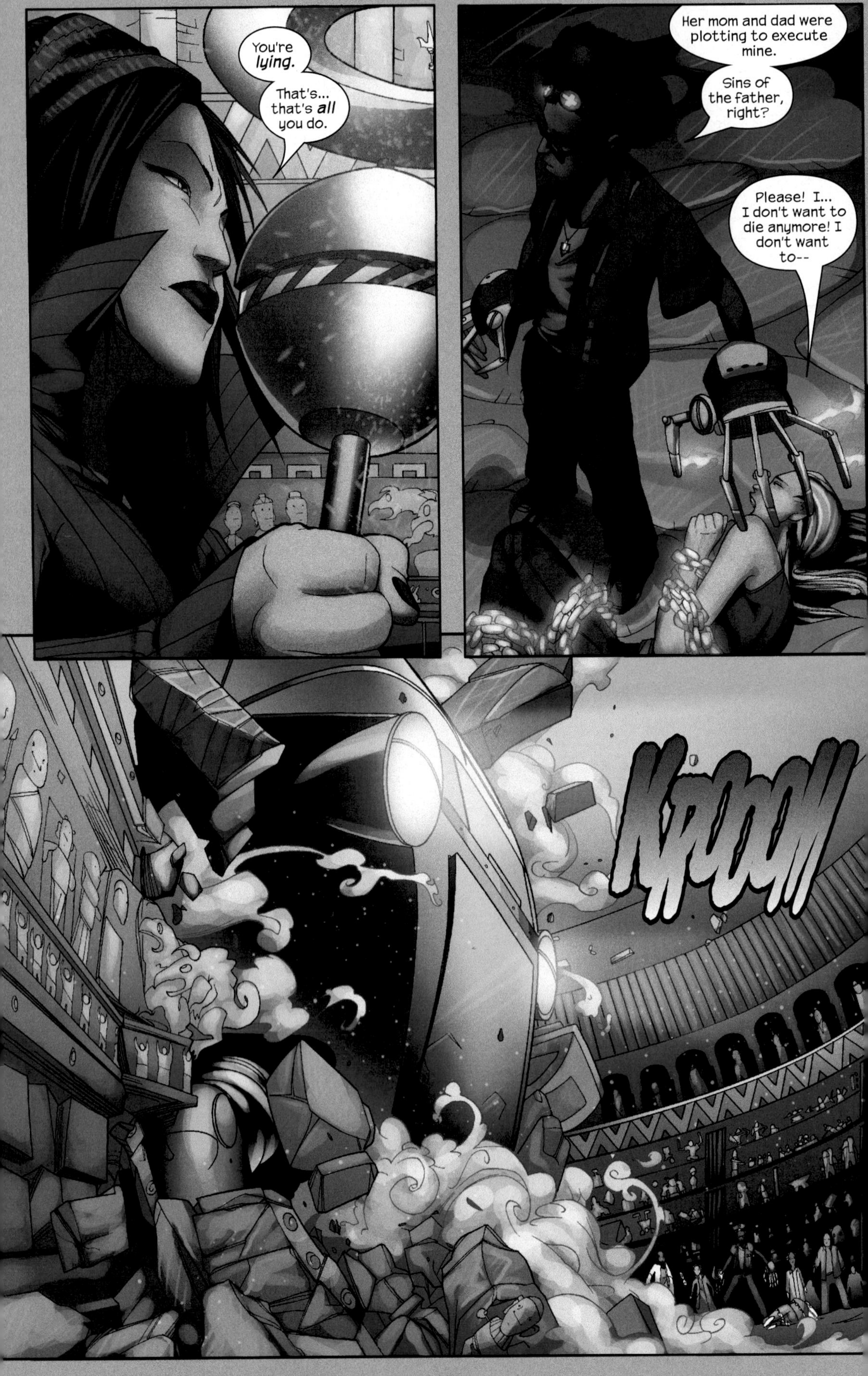
You're *lying.*
That's... that's *all* you do.
Her mom and dad were plotting to execute mine.
Sins of the father, right?
Please! I... I don't want to die anymore! I don't want to--
KROOM

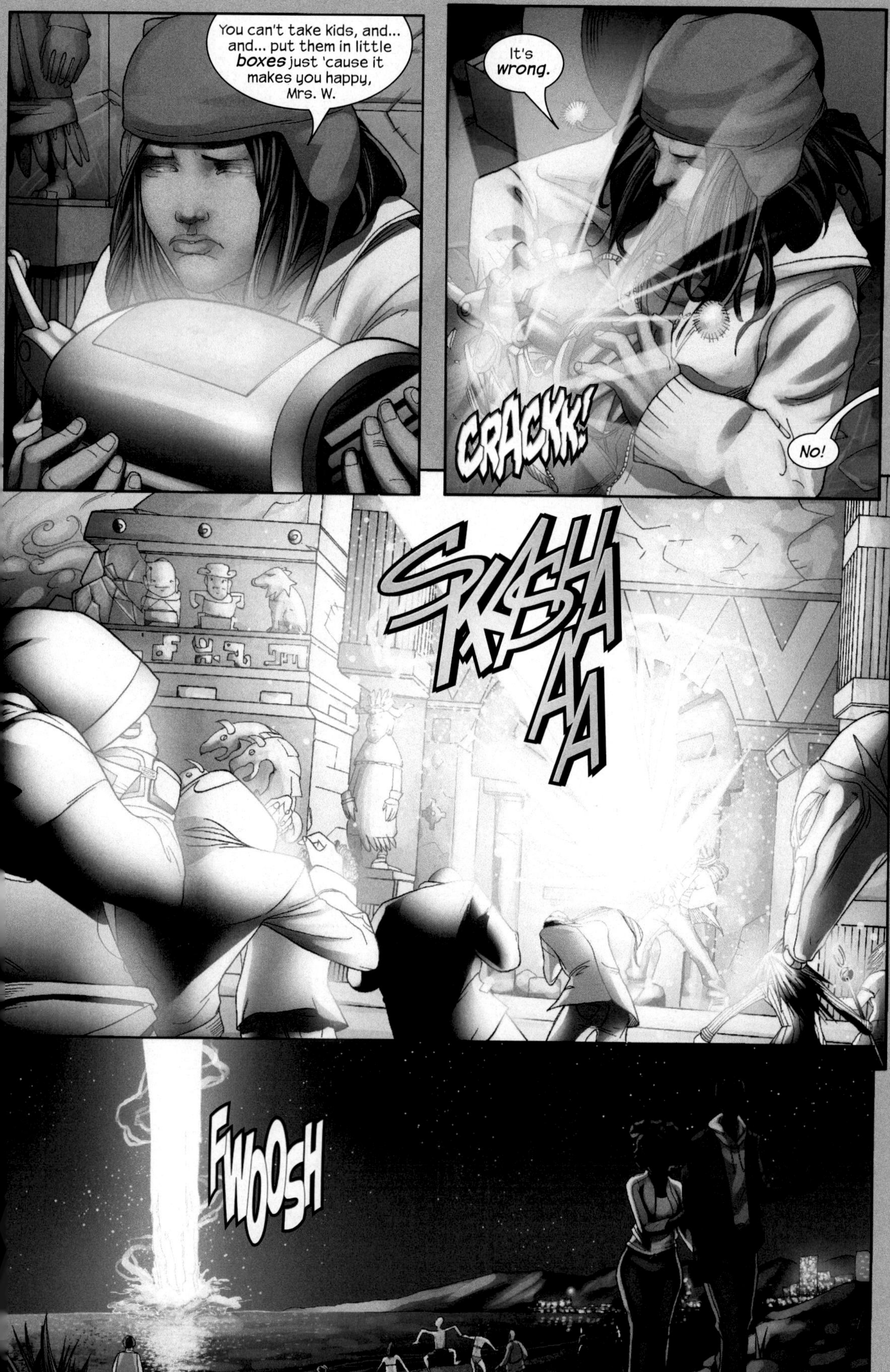
You can't take kids, and... and... put them in little *boxes* just 'cause it makes you happy, Mrs. W.
It's *wrong.*
CRACKK!
No!
SKASHAAA
FWOOSH

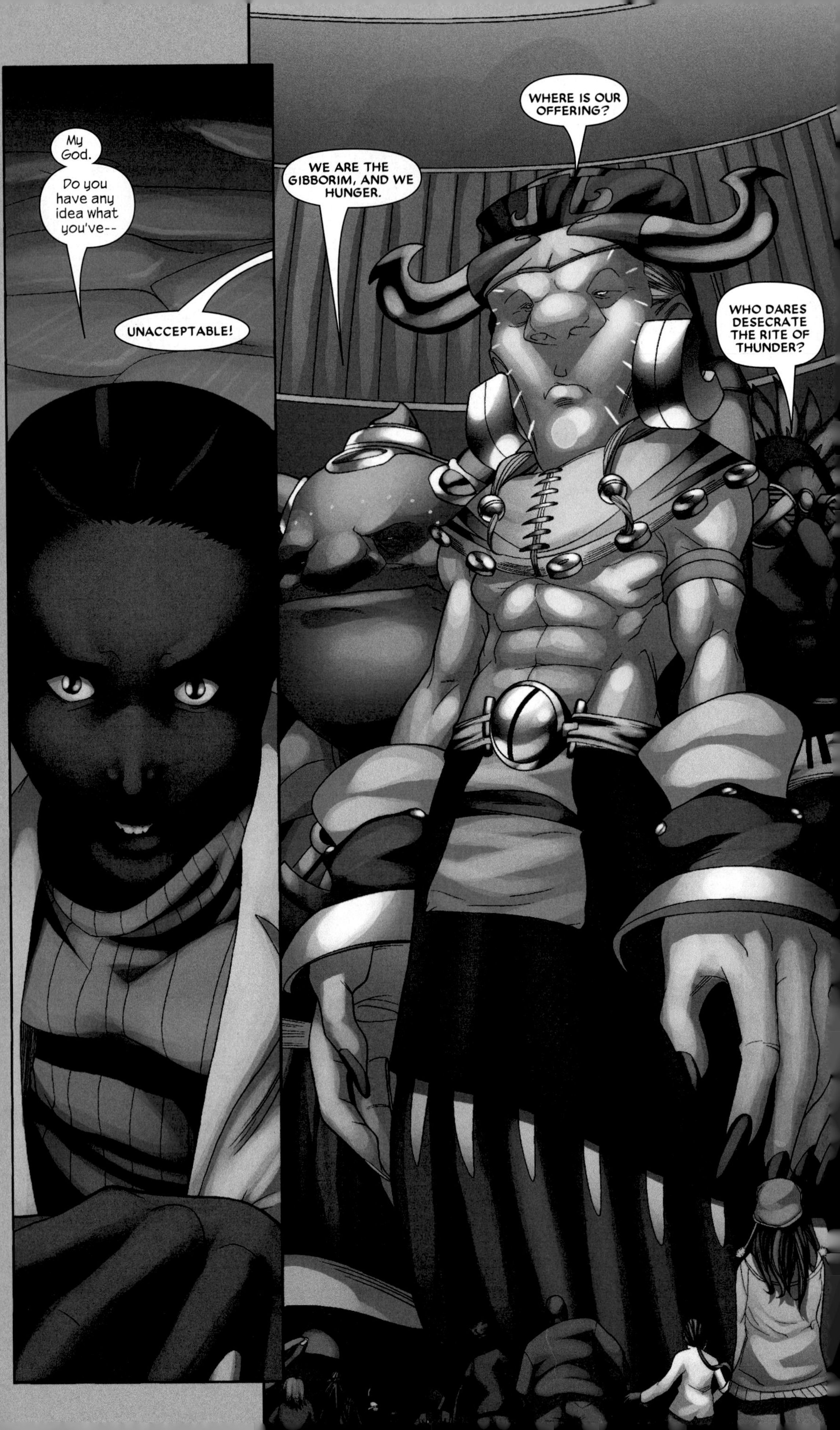
My God.
Do you have any idea what you've--
UNACCEPTABLE!
WE ARE THE GIBBORIM, AND WE HUNGER.
WHERE IS OUR OFFERING?
WHO DARES DESECRATE THE RITE OF THUNDER?

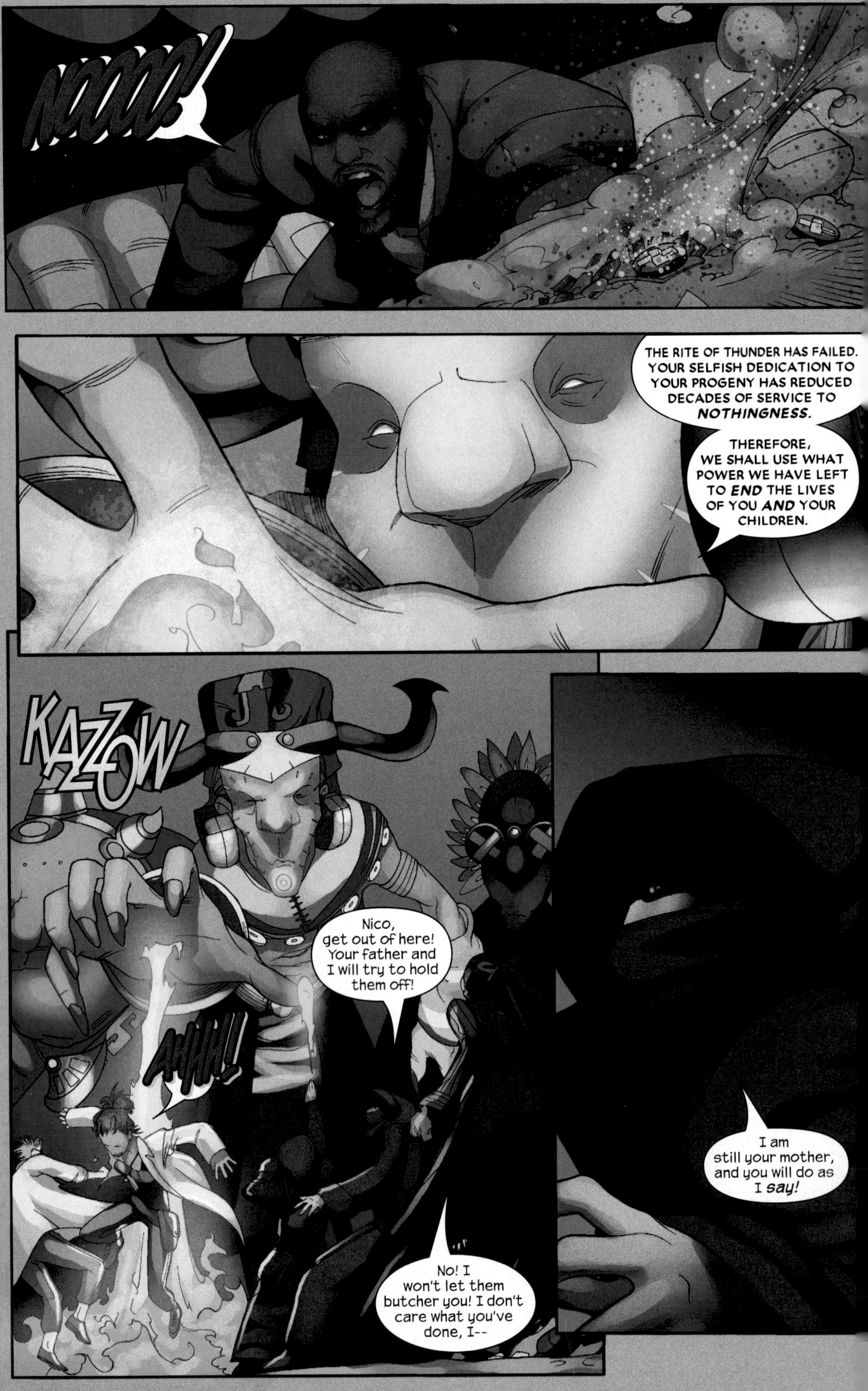
NOOOO!
THE RITE OF THUNDER HAS FAILED. YOUR SELFISH DEDICATION TO YOUR PROGENY HAS REDUCED DECADES OF SERVICE TO NOTHINGNESS.
THEREFORE, WE SHALL USE WHAT POWER WE HAVE LEFT TO END THE LIVES OF YOU AND YOUR CHILDREN.
KAZZOW
Nico, get out of here! Your father and I will try to hold them off!
AHHH!!
No! I won't let them butcher you! I don't care what you've done, I--
I am still your mother, and you will do as I say!

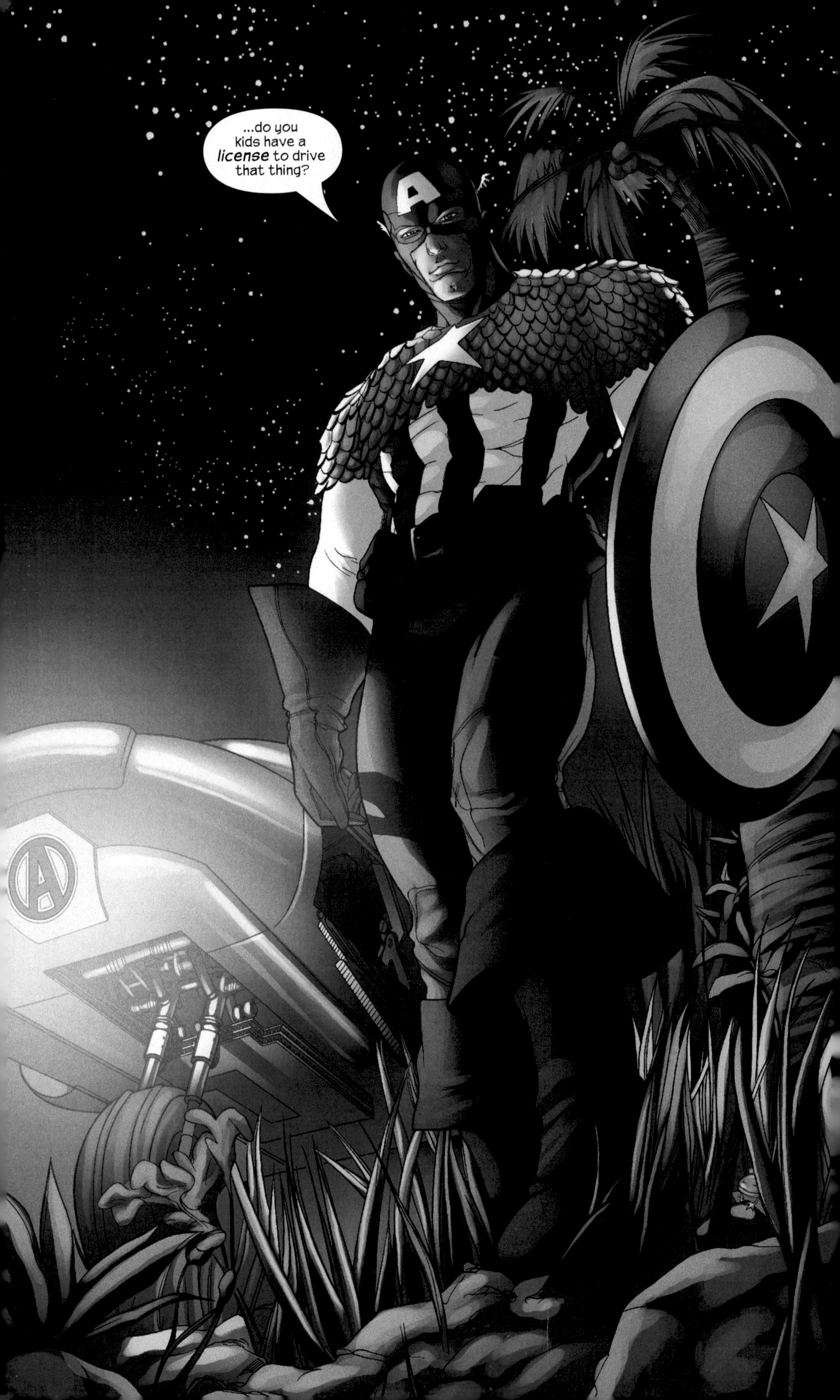
...do you kids have a *license* to drive that thing?

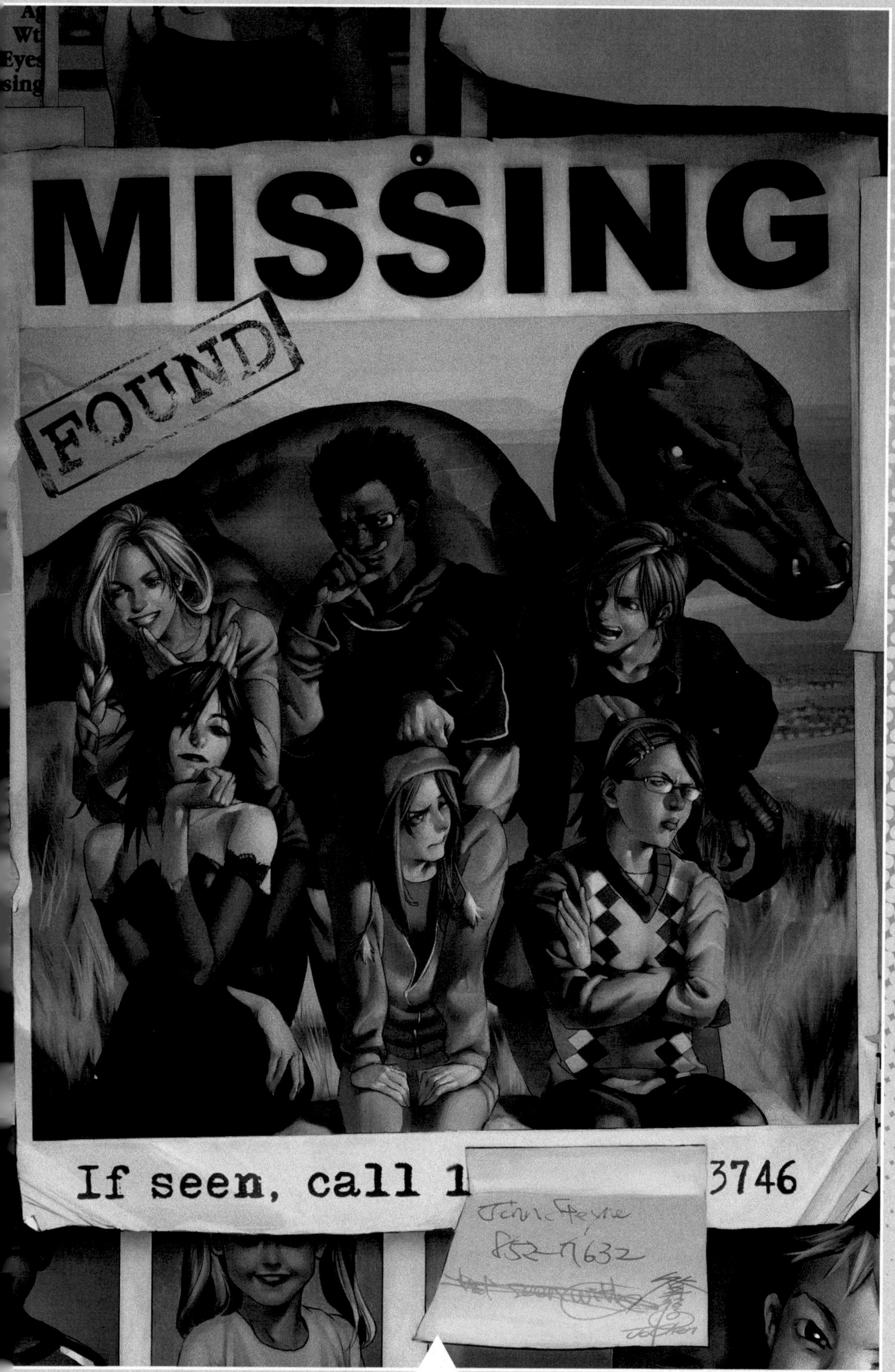
MISSING
FOUND
If seen, call 1
3746

At least once during our adolescent years, many of us felt that our parents were the most *evil* people alive...

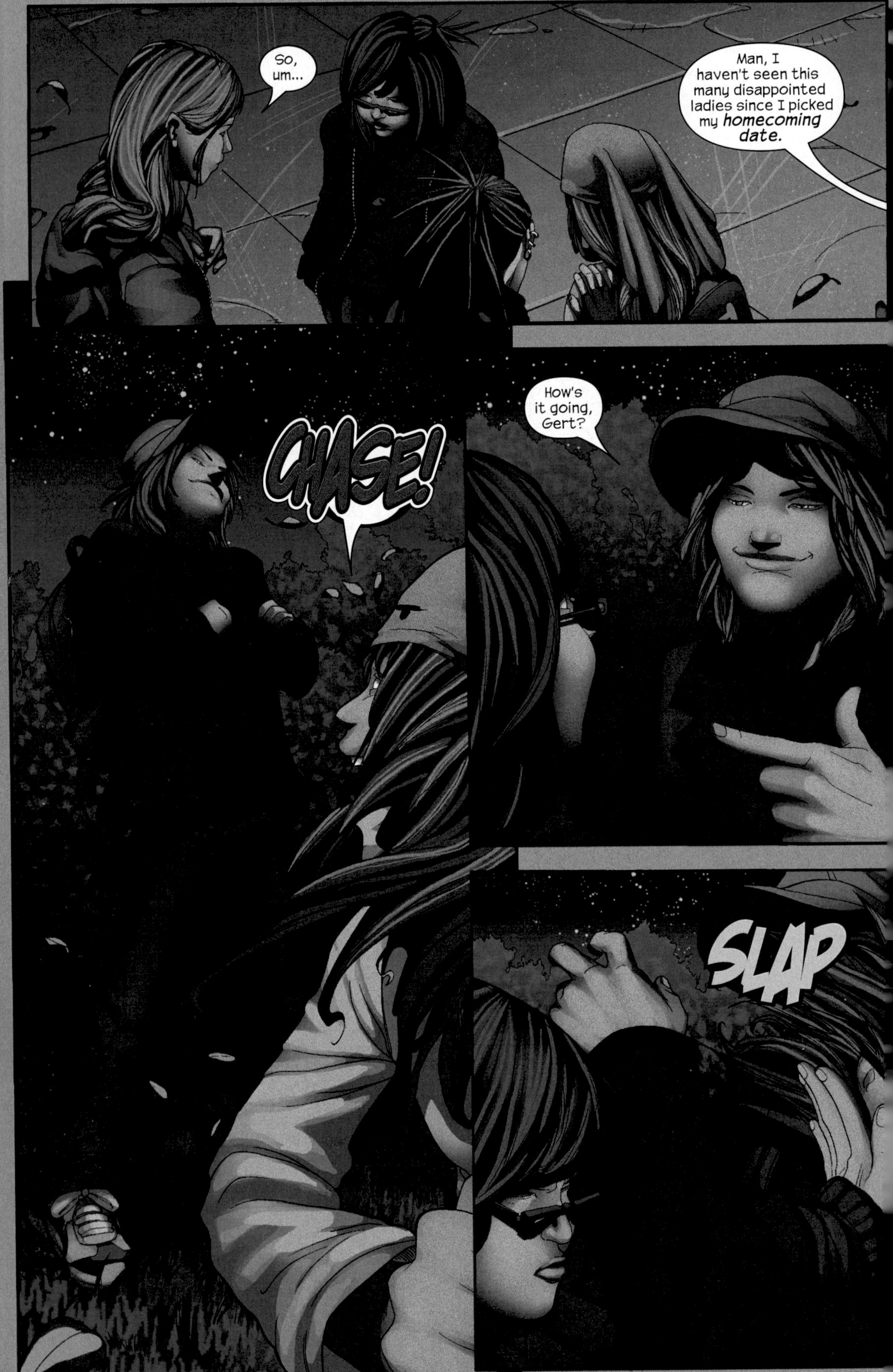
So, um...
Man, I haven't seen this many disappointed ladies since I picked my *homecoming* *date.*
CHASE!
How's it going, Gert?
SLAP

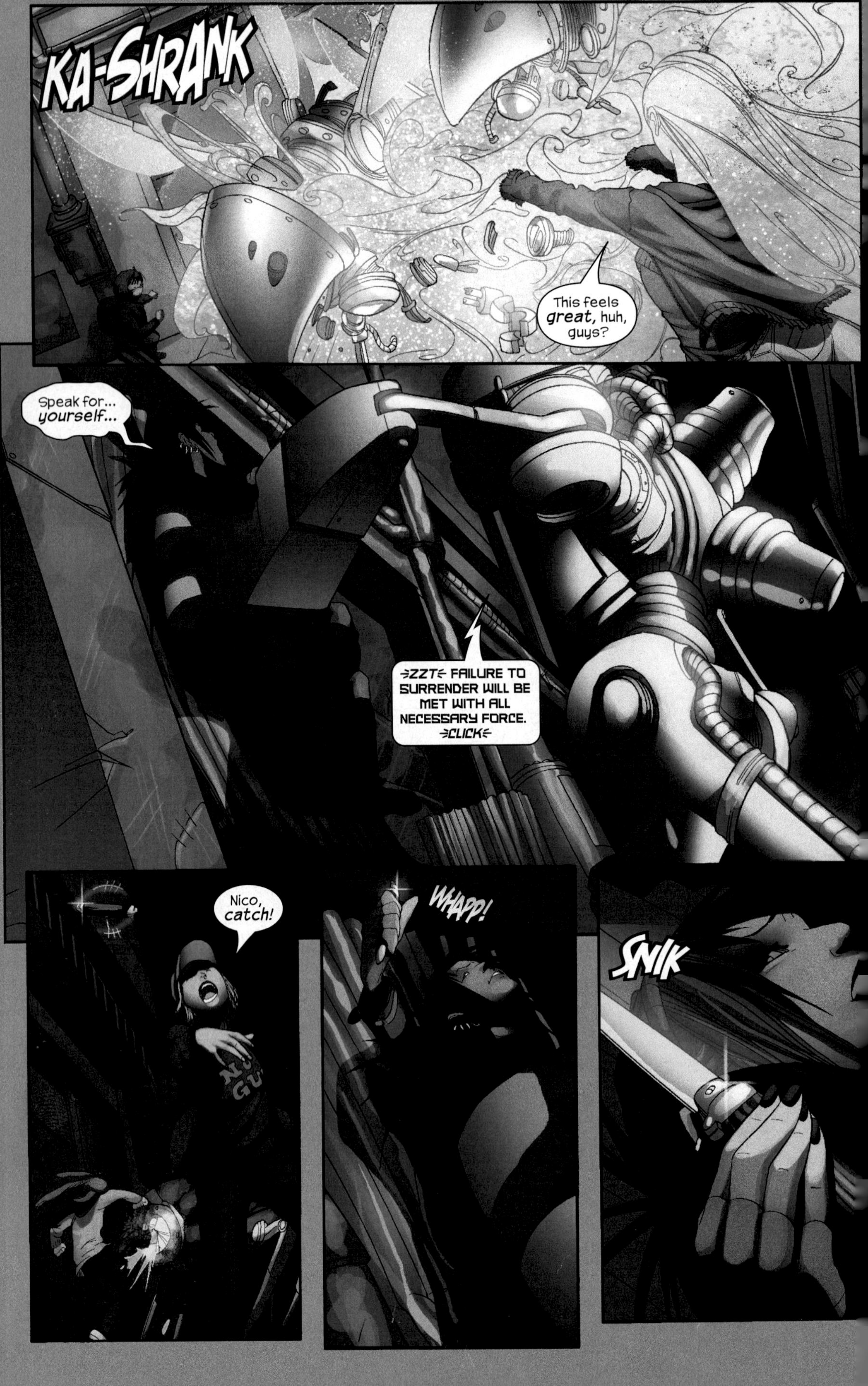
KA-SHRANK
This feels great, huh, guys?
Speak for... yourself...
⋺ZZT⋲ FAILURE TO SURRENDER WILL BE MET WITH ALL NECESSARY FORCE. ⋺CLICK⋲
Nico, catch!
WHAPP!
SNIK

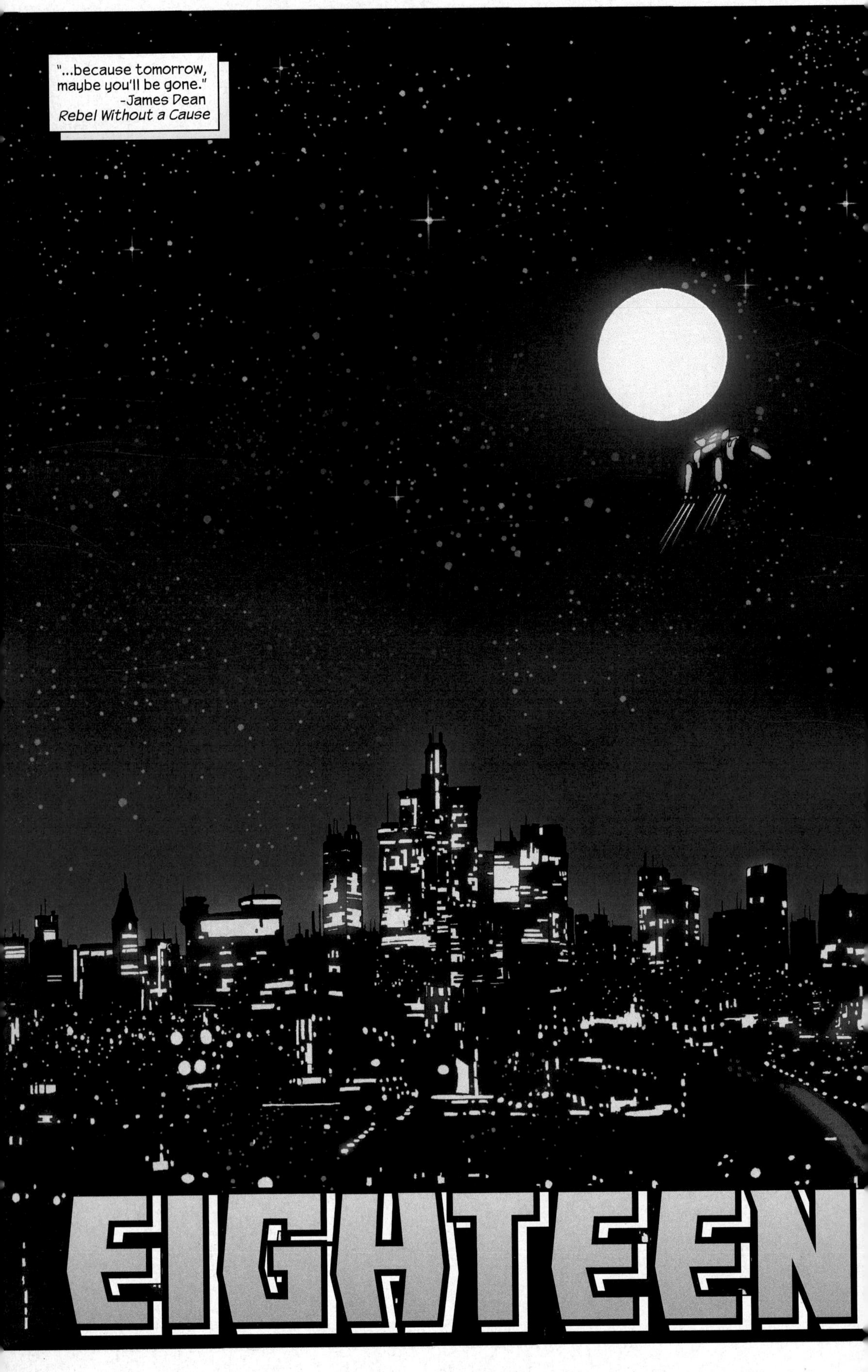
"...because tomorrow, maybe you'll be gone."
-James Dean
Rebel Without a Cause
EIGHTEEN

THIS LETTER APPEARED IN *RUNAWAYS #18*, FOLLOWED BY BRIAN K. VAUGHAN'S RESPONSE:

Team Runaways,

Last issue? What do you mean, **LAST ISSUE**? What the hell does that mean? Did you type it wrong? Were you thinking of something else, like maybe the Sub-Mariner or the Smurfs? How can there be a last issue when the story is obviously going to continue for years? You're some kind of wrong person. Have it looked into.

Your fan,
Joss Whedon

Yep, that's the real Joss Whedon, of BUFFY, ASTONISHING X-MEN *and, uh,* ROSEANNE *fame. Cool, huh? But thanks to the vocal support of loyal readers like you (and Joss), I am thrilled to announce that this is NOT the last issue of Runaways. Our kids are going on a well-deserved vacation for a few short months, but the entire creative team will be bringing them back in early 2005 for* RUNAWAYS #1*! One chapter in the lives of our young heroes has ended, but an all-new, all-different one is about to begin.*

THANK YOU NOTE FROM CHRISTINA STRAIN

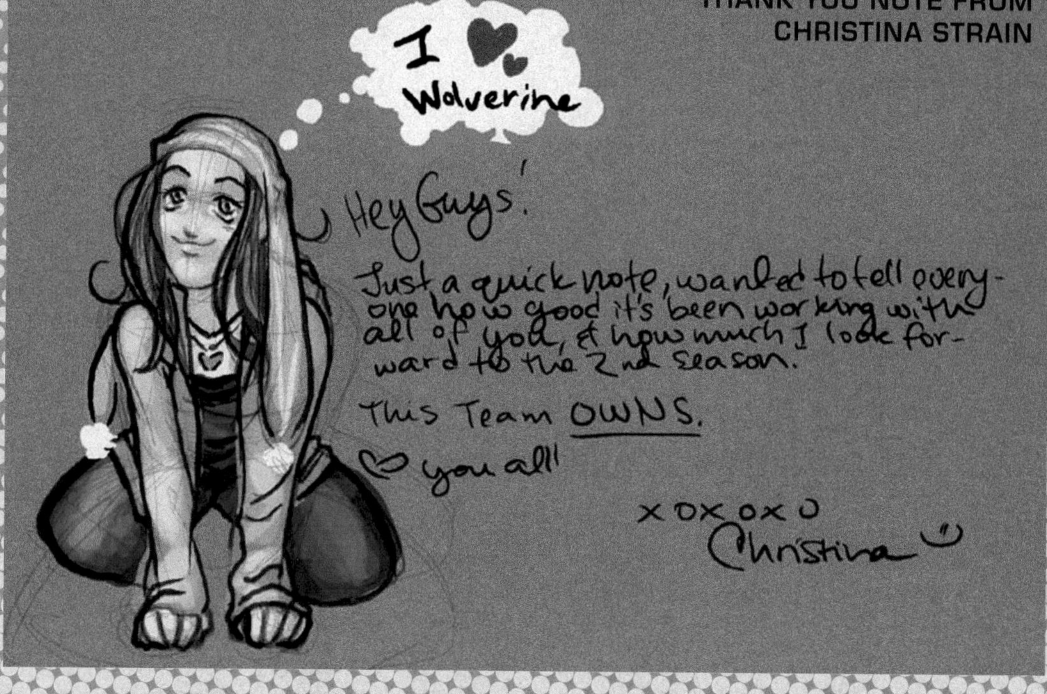

I ♥ Wolverine
Hey Guys!
Just a quick note, wanted to tell every-one how good it's been working with all of you, & how much I look for-ward to the 2nd season.
This Team OWNS.
♥ you all!
xoxoxo
Christina

ADRIAN ALPHONA SKETCHBOOK

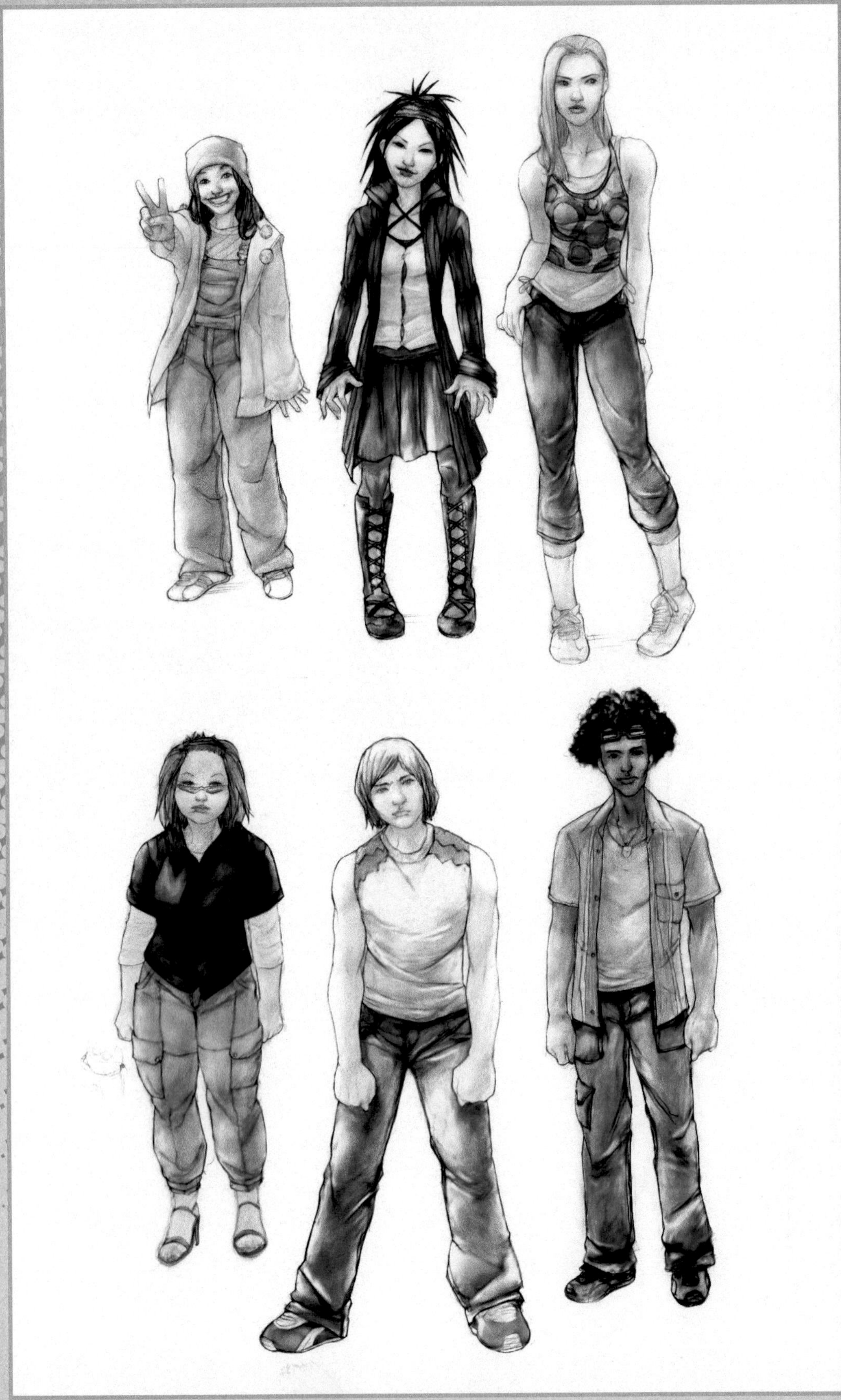

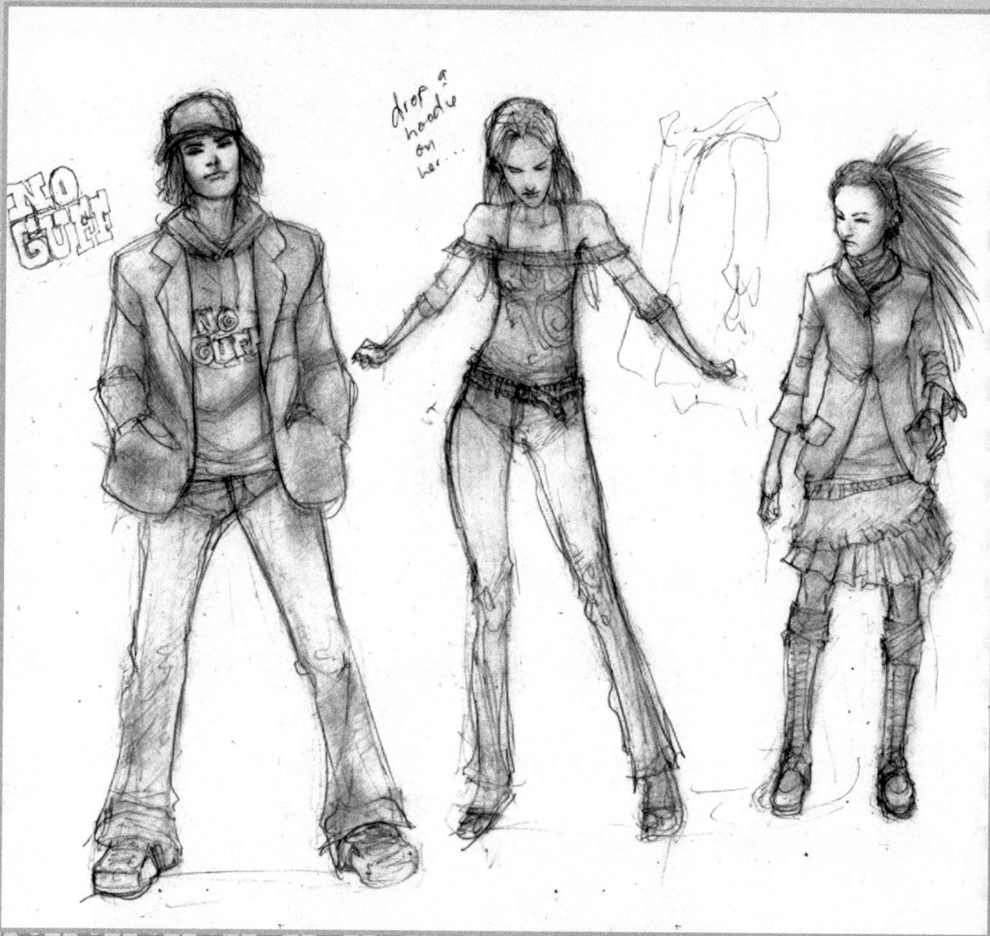
NO GUFF
NO GUFF
drop a hoodie on her...

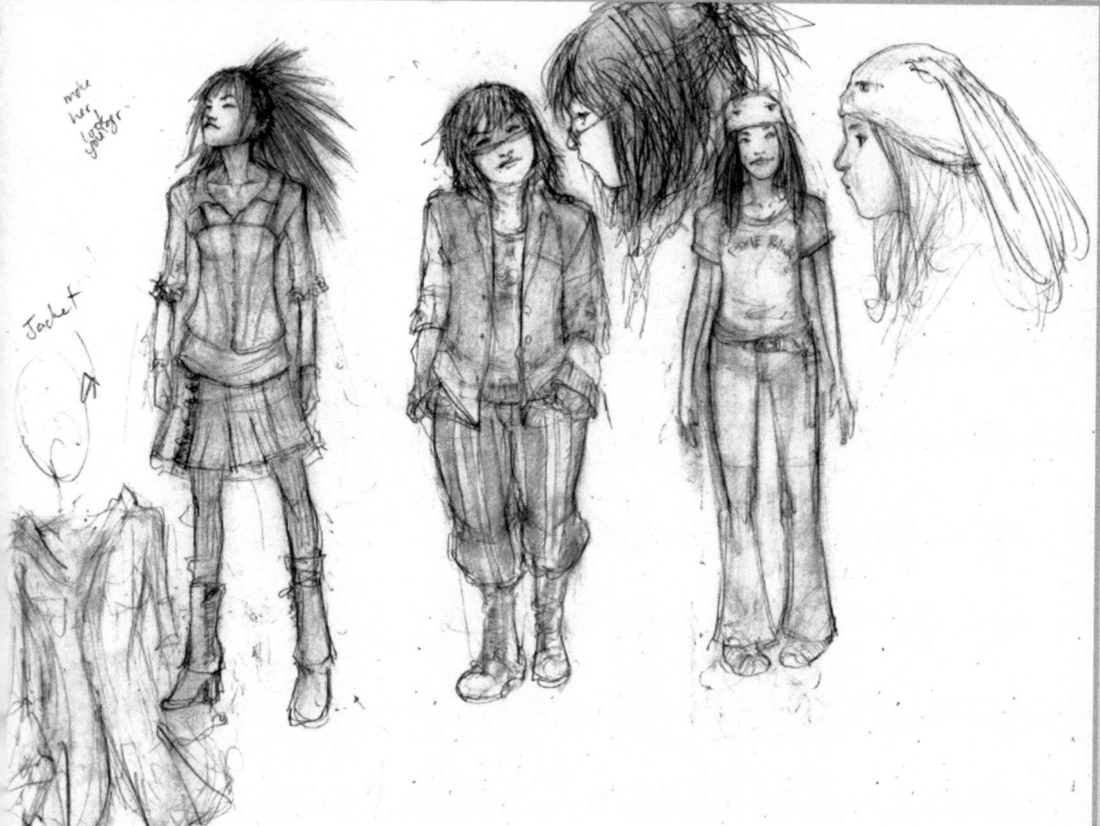
make her look younger
Jacket

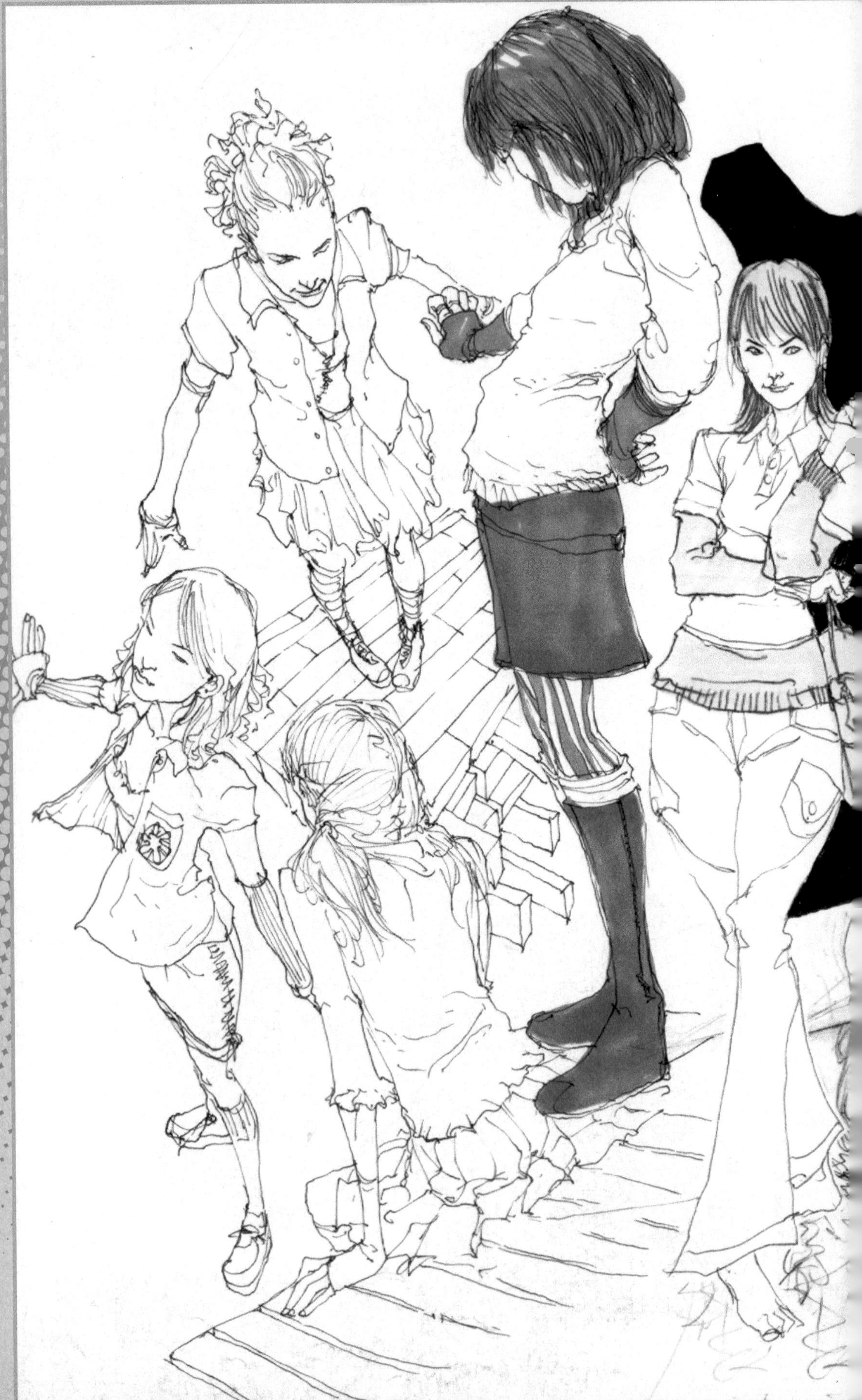

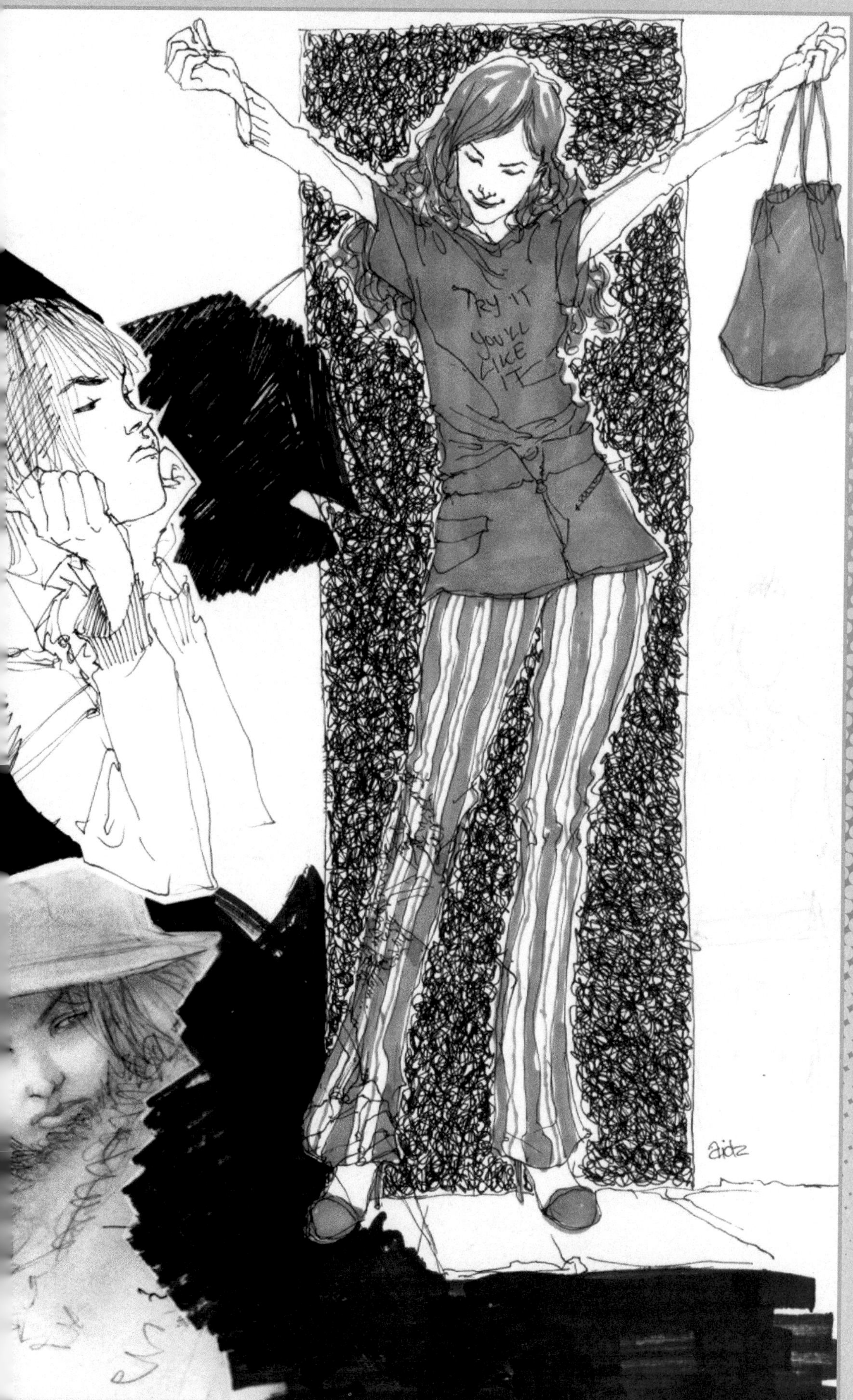
TRY IT YOU'LL LIKE IT
aidz

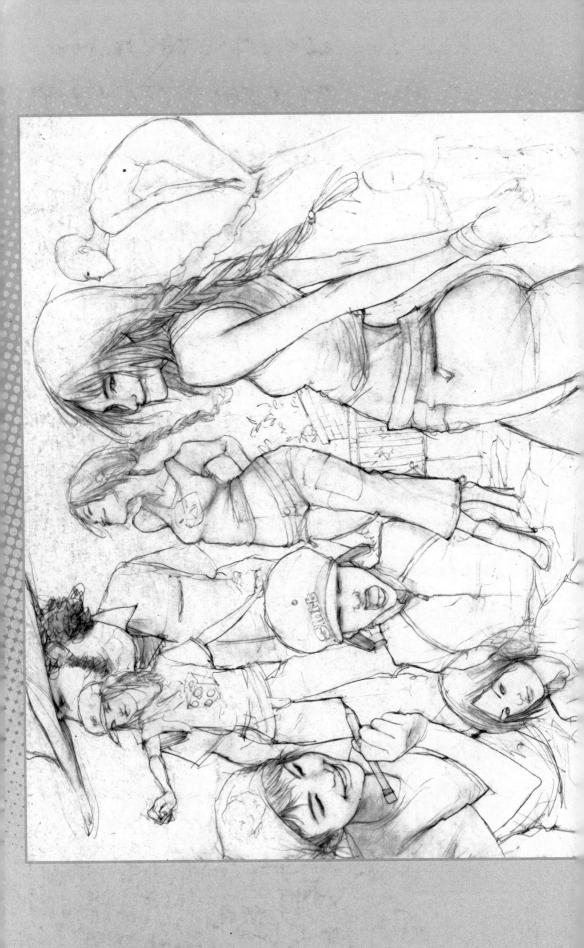